The Believer's Triumph,
Christ living in me.

by D. Michael Cotten

ISBN:979-8-218-04696-5

Contact the Author at

Dmichaelcotten@att.net

Author of exciting books about Jesus Christ

And "GOD, the Holy Spirit".

Purpose for this book.

The theme of this book is to consider for Believers the life we see in the Apostle Paul's statement "It is not I, that lives, but Christ lives in me". We will explore the incredible picture of the early church, before there was a Bible, Believers being "One with GOD", "Worship as a way of life.", the Lord's "Words to live by", the "Circle of Grace", and finally living through Christ living in Believers. Listen as the Apostle Paul explains Christ living in himself.

Galatians 2:20 I have been crucified with Christ. It is no longer I who live, but Christ who lives in me. And the life I now live in the flesh I live by the faith "of" the Son of God, who loved me and gave himself for me. KJV

Philippians 3:9-10 And be found in him, not having mine own righteousness, which is of the law, but that which is through the faith of Jesus Christ, the righteousness which is of God by faith: that I may know Him and the power of His resurrection and the fellowship of His sufferings, being made conformable to His death.

It is true that we put faith in Jesus Christ, or trust in Him for salvation and its benefits. But it is not "our faith" that justifies Believers, it is our faith in the faith of Jesus Christ. It was the faith of Jesus in His Father's love, that allowed him to go to the cross for Believers. This fact helps Believers depend on what Jesus has done and not on what Believers can do. **Jesus has finished the action of sacrifice and believed GOD for resurrection**; Believers trust and receive what the Lord's faith has already obtained for us. Now is the time, we need to believe GOD and His word, and not believe in GOD.

Do you remember, the bracelet "WWJD" <u>What would Jesus do</u>? Knowing GOD's plan for your day or for the next moment is the right focus for daily living, but a relationship with Jesus Christ is not lived in a part-time fashion. Allowing your life to be, "Christ living in you" is the abundant life dimension. <u>Christ living in you</u> starts with you being able to hear GOD speak to you through your Spirit or His word or from "GOD, the Holy Spirit". Once a Believer is committed to acting in faith according to a word from GOD, the confidence to follow Jesus is compelling. Remember what Mary, the Mother of Jesus said to the servants at the Wedding in Cana when wine was needed, "Whatever Jesus says, <u>do it</u>." Those are good words for believers today, also.

The most significant obstacle to "Christ living in you" is losing your focus on Christ and finding your focus on you. Think about the words of Jesus before he went to the cross, "Do not be anxious about the needs of your body or what will be needed tomorrow but seek first <u>the Kingdom of GOD</u> and his righteousness and all the needs of the world will be added unto you. Listen to Jesus.

Matthew 6:31-34 Therefore do not be anxious, saying, <u>what shall we eat? or what shall we drink? or with what shall we be clothed?</u> For the nations <u>seek after all these things</u>. For your heavenly Father knows that you have need of all these things. But <u>seek first the kingdom of God and His righteousness; and all these things shall be added to you.</u> Therefore, do not be anxious about tomorrow; for tomorrow shall be anxious for its own things. Sufficient to the day *is* the evil of it.

Jesus said, "My sheep hear my voice, and I know them, and they follow me." Our first activity "daily" is to open our day to the Father's creation through the love of our Savior and Brother, in the presence of "GOD, the Holy Spirit" and seek the will of GOD for the day. GOD designed the world and its systems, from the bonds of love for the world and mankind. GOD made the Believers Spirit in His image, and they operate according to GOD's word. Our first activity is to seek first the voice of our King and His Kingdom and follow Him through His word and through His Spirit.

All acts of sin come from "the one act" of **not believing on** and **resting in relationship with Jesus**.

Definitions

<u>**Gospel**</u> as used by Jesus and the Apostle Paul has a vastly different meaning from "Good News". The Gospel according to Jesus and the Apostle Paul is "Great News"; but is better described as "<u>At the appointed time</u>, GOD sent the blessed seed (singular) of Abraham to be the blessing for all ethnicities in the world, for the Messiah has come to finish the transgression and to make an end of sins, and to make atonement for iniquity, and to bring in everlasting righteousness, and to seal up the vision and prophecy, to anoint the Most Holy altar in Heaven, to send men and women into the world as a witness of the resurrection event, to send "GOD, the Holy Spirit" to all who believe and ask, reconciling to GOD a people for His new Covenant and the condemning of all sin by GOD. The Gospel is, **"the almost too good to believe good news of all time"**.

The Greek word for Salvation or saved is also the same for word used for <u>delivered</u>, <u>protected</u>, <u>healed</u>, <u>made well</u>, or **made whole**. The Greek words are sozo, soteria, and sodzo and are better characterized as "Total Wellbeing for Believers".

<u>**Grace**</u> came though Jesus Christ and is a love gift for salvation to those who believe in Jesus and Father GOD who sent Him. Grace is also a love gift for a Believers found at the Throne of Grace when there is a time of need for a Believer's weakness to finish the plan of GOD.

Table of Contents

Words from the Author about Writing Style

This book is **<u>not</u>** written in strict adherence to grammatical rules. The Bible and concepts of GOD are complicated. To unpack the compound sentences in the Bible and the interaction of the visible and invisible world; each page will contain highlights, capital letters, quotes, underlines, and cascading verses, to add sound and definition to the words.

Chapter 1

The history of the Christian congregation,
<u>before there was a Bible</u>, is a story to
build faith in Believers through eyewitnesses
to the power of the Resurrection.

Once upon a time, <u>before</u> there was a Bible, the very fact, a man forecast his own death, burial, and resurrection and rose from the dead on the third day and was seen by hundreds of eyewitnesses, <u>was proof</u>, **Jesus was, who He said, He was.** The resurrection of Jesus Christ was an event, so profound, it was enough to build a congregation of Believers across the world in staggering numbers. Witnesses to the resurrection and the words and deeds of Jesus Christ spread around the world <u>in a very short time frame, without a Bible</u>.

At Jesus death, there were no Christians because there was no Christ, there was no Bible, there was no Messiah, there was no hope. Every word Jesus had spoken, taught, claimed, and associated with prophecy <u>was dead</u> and <u>everyone expected Him to stay dead</u>. It is "GOD, the Holy Spirit" **raising Jesus from the dead** that gives power to Christianity because **<u>there is a Christ</u>, <u>the Messiah did come</u>,** AND **Jesus was and is GOD**. There is a <u>Father GOD with a plan</u>, whose <u>Holy Spirit abides with Believers</u>, right now on earth, and **Jesus is alive**.

It is not the Bible, <u>as remarkable as the Bible is</u>, that is the power of the gospel of Jesus Christ. It is the resurrection of Jesus, our Savior, that makes this story so remarkable. **Our GOD is alive!** Without the resurrection there would be no story to tell. No reason for Matthew, Luke, John and

Peter through John Mark to go to the difficult and expensive task to write anything about a carpenter's son, from a small town in the middle of nowhere, before there was paper, pen, and ink.

Four men, who were eyewitnesses, wrote or dictated a record of the life of Jesus Christ, his life of love, service, and His miraculous deeds. Each writer records different or personal aspects to the history of a Carpenter's son, who turned the world "right side up". None of these men knew there would be a Bible.

Jesus, by being born of woman through the seed of GOD's word, gave us an example of an incredible life of love, words of life, miraculous deeds, and then, willingly laid down His life, so through his death, burial, and resurrection the world might be reconciled to GOD. The resurrection proved to Believers, who He was, and who we are, because of who He is.

Listen to Luke describe the confidence Believers can have in the record of his account of the life in Christ Jesus.

Luke 1:1-4 **Since many** took in hand to draw up an account concerning the matters which have been borne out among us, even as those who from *the* beginning delivered to us, becoming eye-witnesses and ministers of the Word, it seemed good to me also, **following all things accurately from the very first**, to write to you **in order**, most excellent Theophilus, so that **you might know the certainty** of those things in which you have been instructed.

Matthew, Mark, Luke, and John recorded the events of the Life of Jesus, not as part of the Bible. Each account was just an individual record of the life and ministry of The Messiah. No one knew there would ever be "The Bible". The Bible would be put together several hundred years later. The foretold resurrection of Jesus Christ was such an event that these men who had deserted Jesus when he died, <u>realized the Divinity of His life</u> **when Jesus was resurrected**. Each writer recorded what they had seen and heard, due to the gravity of this moment in time. Listen to the reason John wrote this report on the life and love of Jesus Christ.

John 20:30-31 And truly Jesus did many other signs in the presence of His disciples (and congregation), which are not written in this record. <u>But these are recorded so</u> **that you might believe that Jesus is the Christ** (The Messiah), <u>the Son of God</u>, and **that believing you might <u>have life in His name.</u>**

**Eternal life with GOD starts at Salvation,
not death of the body.**

In the history of the world, there is **not** another person who can be named who has verifiable documented proof of their life before paper and pen with original documents as this carpenter's son. Not many historians, if any, deny the life of Jesus Christ and his born-again experience. These records are four or more, current to the time, eyewitness reports of the resurrection event, <u>which is the cornerstone of our faith in our Savior and Redeemer</u>. Why is it important that there are four separate records of the resurrection, and why is it the foundation of our faith for the congregation of Believers in Jesus Christ? Answer: If just one of these records is true, we can be saved through the words and actions of Jesus Christ, <u>but the truth is there are four independent records of the life of Messiah</u>. The plan of GOD for our reconciliation to Father GOD, happened. Our Savior **is alive** and loves the world and will be as large a part of each Believer's life as the Believer chooses.

It is not the Bible that offers salvation and all its benefits, it is the resurrection of Jesus having laid down His life and having been raised from the dead by "GOD, the Holy Spirit" that changed the world and every Believer's life. Eternal life is ours, because Jesus is alive in Believers, and **because He lives inside us**, we must address the world from His perspective and not from what we see, hear, taste, touch, smell, or feel.

Very soon after the sharing of Matthews record of Jesus as The Messiah, with all the Torah references and Prophecy fulfillment from the Torah, Christians started using what we call the Old Covenant or Testament as scripture and **confirmation of Jesus Christ, as The Messiah**.

The Old Covenant or Testament

When the Christians discovered that the Torah was a record of the prophecies of the coming Messiah and that Jesus fulfilled the details of the prophecies, GOD's feast days, the Temple furniture, and more, the congregations began using the Torah as their own scripture in their assemblies. The detail of the coming of Jesus Christ in the Torah was more evidence of GOD's plan to redeem mankind. It was evident, that GOD had founded a people who would bless the entire world through a Savior. The proof of who Jesus was, and who He would be, explained who Believers would be, because of **who Jesus is**.

Specifically, Matthew's record of the life of Jesus Christ is filled front to back with prophecies from the Torah that came to fruition in Jesus Christ, the Messiah's Life, death, and resurrection.

In Matthew's Gospel we read, John, the Baptist fulfilled the prophecies in *Isaiah 40:3*, that there would be a prophet in the wilderness that would announce the arrival of the Messiah.

John, the Baptist would look like and have a ministry like Elijah. In *Matthew 11:10*, Jesus quoted from Malachi 3:1 proving that John, the Baptist was the fulfillment of the promised messenger **who would make straight the way for Jesus**. Also in *Malachi 4:5-6,* the prophet predicted that God would send a messenger like Elijah. Think about this, Isaiah had predicted this over 700 years before Christ, and Malachi wrote it about 450 years before Jesus came.

In *Matthew 1:18-25*, we read the account of the birth of Jesus. His mother Mary was a virgin, and the angel appeared to Joseph to explain that Mary was with child by "GOD, the Holy Spirit". This was the fulfillment of what Isaiah 7:14 "Behold the virgin shall be with child and bear a son and they shall call Him Immanuel which means, God with us". Now we know from Matthew 2:23 and Luke 1:26-28 that Joseph and Mary were from Nazareth in the Galilean area but the prophet Micah had predicted 450 years before that The Messiah would be born in Bethlehem in Micah 5:2. We read in Luke's account of the Lord's birth that Joseph and Mary had to go register in Joseph's family hometown of Bethlehem and while they were there, Jesus was born. Who could have foreseen that coming, but God?

And at this time, there is still no idea that there will ever be a Bible. The resurrection of Jesus and the power of being One with "GOD, the Holy Spirit" spread the life-giving message of a risen Savior throughout the world. It was the testimonies of people affected by Jesus, GOD, the Holy Spirit, and his followers that carried the message, with power, before there was a Bible.

The Christian Savior is a living GOD, He is "The Messiah" who eliminated the penalty of sin and announced the benefits of salvation for all who believe **and** put Jesus on the throne of their life. Listen to and look at the picture of Jesus from a Prophecy from Isaiah, a Psalm from David, and a word from the Apostle Paul.

Isaiah 53:4-6 Surely, He has borne our griefs, and carried our sorrows; yet we esteemed Him stricken, smitten of God, and afflicted. But He *was* wounded for our transgressions; *He was* bruised for our iniquities; the chastisement of our peace *was* on Him; and with His stripes we ourselves are healed. All we like sheep have gone astray; we have turned, each one to his own way; and Jehovah has laid on Him the iniquity of us all.

Psalms 103:2-5 **Bless Jehovah**, O my soul, and **forget not all His benefits**; who **forgives** all your iniquities; who **heals** all your diseases; who **redeems** your life from ruin; who **crowns** you *with* loving-kindness and tender mercies; who **satisfies** your mouth with good; your **youth is renewed** like the eagle's.

1st Corinthians 15:1-8 And, brothers, I declare to you the gospel (the good news of the coming of the Messiah for the world) which I preached to you, which also you have received, and in which you stand; by which you also are being kept safe, if you hold fast to the word which I preached to you, unless you believed in vain.

For I delivered to you first, of all that (Gospel) which I also received, that **Christ died for our sins**, according to the Scriptures, and that **He was buried, and that He rose again the third day** according to the Scriptures; and that He was seen by Cephas, (Peter) then by the Twelve. Afterward He was seen by over five hundred brothers at once, of whom the greater part remains until this present day, but also some fell asleep.

Afterward He was seen by James, then by all the apostles. And **last of all He was seen by me also**, as one born out of time.

Before there was a Bible, Father GOD's plan of the resurrection of His son, was such an event that it transformed the world and your life and mine. Did you see the prophecy in each scripture assuring Believers this was and is GOD's plan. The Lord's "saving grace to be born-again" **was given before we were born and while we were yet sinners**. And this salvation is much greater than a ticket to heaven it is **"a way of life" in Christ Jesus** with the power of the resurrection inside each Believer. **The Kingdom of GOD being inside Believers** allows us to live from the inside out and not be subject to earthly wisdom and emotions from outside. Listen as the Apostle Paul describes, "We are saved by **His life**".

The Apostle Paul knew the Torah and the prophecies of the Messiah, and when he met the resurrected Jesus on the road to Damascus, Paul became a Jesus follower in the blink of his eyes. Read about Paul being blinded in his encounter with Jesus in Acts 9:1-18

Romans 5:8-11 But God commends His love toward us in that while **we were, yet sinners Christ died for us**. Much more then, being now justified by His blood, we shall be saved from wrath through Him. For if *when* **we were enemies**, we were reconciled to God through the death of His Son, much more, being reconciled, **we shall be saved by His life**. And not only *so*, but we also rejoice in God through our Lord Jesus Christ, **by whom we have now received the reconciliation (with GOD).**

Very important point, Believers were reconciled to GOD through the death and resurrection of GOD's son, but we will be victorious in this world <u>by His life and His instructions</u>. **It is the Believer accepting the Spirit of Jesus Christ, "GOD, the Holy Spirit" Immanuel, "GOD with us" that makes Believers "One with GOD"**. If Jesus was filled with "GOD, the Holy Spirit" it is important to the Believer's life **that we are filled with "GOD, the Holy Spirit" so that we can be "One with GOD"**. Father GOD has made it easy to receive or know "GOD, the Holy Spirit" by asking, <u>listen to this scripture.</u>

Luke 11:13 "If you then, who are evil, know how to give good gifts to your children, **how much more will the heavenly Father <u>give the Holy Spirit to those who ask him!</u>"**

It is very important for every Believer to focus on the finished works of Jesus, which are <u>1985 years old.</u> The Lord's finished works are **done**; therefore, Believers must know and act on the promises by and through the Spirit to bring them into the present. **Everyone's sins were in the future** for people living after Jesus went to the cross. Listen to these next scriptures by the Apostle Paul of the promises established by Christ Jesus, waiting on Believers to use them.

Romans 8:1-4 There is therefore <u>now</u> "<u>no</u>" condemnation to them which are in Christ Jesus, <u>who walk not after the flesh, but after the Spirit</u>. For the law of **the Spirit of life in Christ Jesus** hath made me <u>free from the law of sin and death</u>. For what the law could not do, in that it was weak through the flesh, <u>God sending his own Son in the likeness of sinful flesh, and for sin, condemned sin in the flesh</u>: **That the righteousness of the law might be fulfilled in us, who walk not after the flesh, but after the Spirit.**

The early followers of Jesus understood this "NOW" freedom of "NO" condemnation of their life in the flesh and early

Believers appeared to have <u>no fear of death because of their</u> <u>Life with Christ and His resurrection.</u>

1st Corinthians 1:30-31 But of Him you are in Christ Jesus, who of God is made to us (Believers) **wisdom and righteousness and sanctification and redemption**; so that, according as it is written, "He who glories, <u>let him glory in *the* Lord.</u>"

Christianity is not a religion made by men <u>to size up their god</u> but a congregation of Believers following a risen Savior, who is offering a relationship with GOD Almighty as Father, Brother, and Friend.

As a conclusion to this section about the Bible, let us hear from Peter, an eyewitness to the "Resurrection", and his description of the importance of the prophetic words from the Old Testament and the Bible to come.

2nd Peter 1:16-21 For we did not follow <u>cleverly devised myths</u> when we made known to you the power and coming of our Lord Jesus Christ, but <u>we were eyewitnesses of his majesty</u>. For when he received honor and glory from God, the Father, and the voice was borne to him by the Majestic Glory, "This is my beloved Son, with whom I am well pleased," we ourselves heard this very voice borne from heaven, for we were with him on the holy mountain.

And <u>we have the prophetic word more fully confirmed</u>, to which you will do well to <u>pay attention as to a lamp shining in a dark place</u>, until the day dawns and the morning star rises in your hearts, <u>knowing this</u> first of all, that no prophecy of Scripture **comes from someone's own interpretation**. <u>For no prophecy was ever produced by the will of man, but **men spoke from God as they were carried along by the Holy Spirit.**</u>

**GOD had a plan to redeem Mankind and
Give Believers, "The New life in Jesus Christ."
through "GOD, the Holy Spirit".**

This next section is John's record of the facts detailing Father GOD's plan of sending Jesus, through the seed of a woman as a man, to reconcile mankind to GOD.

To understand Life in Jesus Christ, we must look at Father GOD who sent Jesus to redeem our lives from death, hell, and the grave. It is Father GOD's desire to have a relationship with Believers on Earth, right now. **Jesus** came to deal with all the things <u>Father GOD hates</u> and show mankind a perfect representation of <u>what mankind filled with the "Nature of GOD" **without sin** would have looked like <u>if Adam and Eve had not broken covenant with GOD</u>. Listen as John describes the evil things that came into the world with sin, and the things GOD despises.

1st John 2:15 <u>Do not love the world or the things in the world</u>. If anyone loves the world, the love of the Father is not in him. For all that is in the world—the <u>desires of the flesh,</u> and the <u>desires of the eyes,</u> and <u>pride of life **are not from the Father**</u> but are from the world.

Can you accept the teachings of Jesus Christ as the fundamental expression of the Father's love and plan, if so, the Believer <u>enters</u> the timeless quality of living which is called "eternal life"? Do you ever wonder if GOD really loves you, **the answer is yes** and the proof is Father GOD sending Jesus to die and suffer GOD's wrath for sin, <u>to redeem you from your "Sin Nature" and give you a New Spirit so Father GOD could send part of Himself in "God, the Holy Spirit" to be inside Believers so GOD could have a relationship with His creation, 24/7</u>.

For GOD <u>so loved</u> the world
That <u>He Gave His Son.</u>

Listen to the Luke and the Apostles John and Paul give us keys to living in the Spirit of Jesus Christ. <u>GOD's plan</u> for the World was to send His Son Jesus Christ baptized with "GOD, the Holy Spirit" to reconcile Believers and offer a new covenant with GOD. The following scriptures lay out the fact <u>that Jesus was sent by Father GOD</u> to die for you and me, it was personal to Father GOD. Listen to the following scriptures to hear and appreciate Father GOD's plan of <u>sending His Son</u> to save the world. Jesus confirms along with the Apostles <u>that Father GOD sent Jesus as the Godhead's plan</u>. Here are a series of scriptures detailing the sending of Jesus as our Savior.

Luke 4:17-19 And there was delivered unto Jesus the book of the prophet Isaiah. And when he had opened the book, he found the place where it was written, The <u>Spirit of the Lord</u> *is* upon me, because he has anointed me to preach the gospel to the poor; **he has sent me** to heal the brokenhearted, to preach deliverance to the captives, and recovering of sight to the blind, to set at liberty them that are bruised, To preach the acceptable year of the Lord. (Isaiah 61)

Luke 9:47-48 But Jesus, knowing the reasoning of their hearts, took a child and put him by his side and said to them, "Whoever receives this child in my name receives me, and <u>whoever receives me</u> **receives him who sent me**. <u>For he who is least among you all,</u> is the one who is great."

John 3:33-36 Whoever receives his testimony (the Gospel) sets his seal to this, that God is true. For **he whom God has sent** utters the words of God, **for he gives the *Holy* Spirit without measure**. The Father loves the Son and has given all things into his hand. **Whoever believes in the Son has eternal life**; whoever <u>does not obey</u> the Son shall not see life, <u>but the wrath of God remains on him</u>.

John 5:30-32 Jesus said, "I can do nothing on my own. As I hear, I judge, and my judgment is just because I seek **not** <u>my own will</u> but **the will of him who sent me**. If I alone bear witness about myself, my testimony is not true. There is another who bears witness about me, and I know that the testimony that he bears about me is true. (John, the Baptist)

John 5:36-40 Jesus speaking to the Pharisees, "But the testimony that I have is greater than that of John (the Baptist) For the works that the Father has given me to accomplish, the very works that I am doing, bear witness about me <u>that</u> **the Father has sent me**. And **the Father who sent me** has himself borne witness about me. His voice you have never heard, his form you have never seen, and you do not have his word abiding in you, for you do not believe **the one whom he has sent**. You search the Scriptures because you think that in them you have eternal life; and <u>it is they that bear witness about me, yet you refuse to come to me that you may have life</u>".

John 6:35-40 Jesus said to them, "**I am the bread of life**; whoever comes to me <u>shall not hunger</u>, and whoever believes in me <u>shall never thirst</u>. But I said to you that you have seen me and <u>yet</u> **do not believe**. All that the Father gives me will come to me, and whoever comes to me I will never cast out. <u>For I have come down from heaven, not to do my own will but</u> **the will of him who sent me**. And this is <u>the will of him</u> **who sent me**, that I should lose nothing of all that he has given me but raise it up on the last day. **For this is the will of my Father**, that <u>everyone who looks on the Son and</u> **believes in him should have eternal life**, and I will raise him up on the last day."

John 6:56-58 Whoever feeds on my flesh and drinks my blood abides in me, and I in him. **As the living Father sent me**, and I live because of the Father, so whoever feeds on me, he also will live because of me. This is the bread that came down from heaven, not like the bread the fathers ate, and died. <u>Whoever feeds on this bread</u> **will live forever."**

John 7:28-30 So Jesus proclaimed, as he taught in the temple, "You know me, and you know where I come from. But I have not come of my own accord. **He who sent me is true**, and him you do not know. I know him, for **I come from him**, and **he sent me**." So, they were seeking to arrest him, but no one laid a hand on him, because his hour had not yet come.

John 6:27-29 Labor not for the meat which perishes, but for that meat which endures unto everlasting life, which the Son of man shall give unto you: for him hath God the Father sealed. Then said they unto him, <u>what shall we do, that we might work the works of God</u>? Jesus answered and said unto them, <u>this is the work of God</u>, **that you believe on him whom he hath sent.**

John 12:44-50 And Jesus cried out and said, "<u>Whoever believes in me, believes not in me</u> but **in him who sent me**. And <u>whoever sees me</u> **sees him who sent me**. I have come into the world as light, so that whoever believes in me may not remain in darkness. If anyone hears my words and does not keep them, I do not judge him; for I did not come to judge the world **but to save the world**. <u>The one who rejects me and does **not** receive my words has a judge; "the word" that I have spoken will judge him on the last day.</u> For I have not spoken on my own authority, **but the Father who sent me has himself given me a commandment—what to say and what to speak**. And I know that his commandment **is eternal life**. What I say, therefore, I say as the **Father has told me.**"

John 13:19 From this time I tell you, before its coming to pass, that, when it may come to pass, <u>you may believe that I am *he*</u> ; verily, verily, I say to you, he who is receiving whomsoever I may send, doth receive me; and <u>he who is receiving me</u>, doth **receives Him who sent me.**

John 15:20-21 Remember the words that I said to you: 'A servant is not greater than his master.' If they persecuted me, they will also persecute you. If they kept my word, they will also keep yours. But all these things they will do to you on account of my name because **they do not know him <u>who sent me</u>**.

John 16:4-6 But I have said these things to you, that when their hour comes you may remember that I told them to you. "I did not say these things to you from the beginning, because I was with you. But now I am going to **<u>him who sent me</u>**, and none of you asks me, 'Where are you going?' But because I have said these things to you, sorrow has filled your heart.

John 17:16-21 (Father) <u>They are not of the world, even as I am not of the world.</u> Sanctify them through Your truth. <u>Your Word is truth.</u> **<u>As You have sent Me into the world</u>**, even so **I have sent them into the world**. And I sanctify Myself for their sakes, so that <u>they also might be sanctified in truth</u>. And I do not pray for these alone, <u>but for those also who shall believe on Me through their word</u>, that **they all may be one, as You, Father, *are* in Me, and I in You**, that **they also may be one in Us, so that the world may believe that <u>You have sent Me.</u>**

John 20:22 When he had said this, he showed them his hands and his side. Then the disciples were glad when they saw the Lord. Jesus said to them again, "Peace be with you. As **<u>the Father has sent me</u>, even so I am sending you**." And when he had said this, he breathed on them and said to them, **<u>"Receive the Holy Spirit"</u>**.

Galatians 4:3-7 In the same way we also, when we were children, were enslaved to the elementary principles of the world. But when the fullness of time had come, **<u>God sent forth his Son</u>, born of woman, born under the law, to redeem** those who were under the law, so that we might receive adoption as sons. And because you are sons, **God has sent the Spirit of his Son into our hearts**, crying, "Abba! Father!" So, you are no longer a slave, but a son, and if a son, <u>then an heir through God.</u>

<u>Believers are now Sons and **GOD is now our Father** and **Jesus is now our brother** and **"GOD, the Holy Spirit"** is our best Friend and seal as Family.</u> Think about it, Jesus was and is the Father's plan for reconciliation of Believers and The Father sending <u>"GOD, the Holy Spirit" to every believer.</u> Jesus is still Immanuel, GOD with us through **sending His Spirit to Believers**. GOD was, is, and will be pulling for you to live and fellowship in His family, as the special person you are, but it is your choice.

The following is a list of the references to all three personifications of the Godhead in a single Scripture or the continuing sentence confirming all aspects of <u>GOD working beyond measure for the Believers benefit</u>. To build on the power of the Resurrection, and the redemption plan of Father GOD, now let us introduce "GOD, the Holy Spirit" **the power for the Believers life in Jesus Christ.** Knowing the three personifications of GOD in the daily life of Christians proclaims GOD's love for Believers.

**References to the Trinity or Godhead
Working for and loving Believers.**

It is amazing to consider how often all three personifications of GOD are trying to love an obstinate people without violating your free-will to choose life with GOD or choose life without GOD. For examples of the Godhead working together to lift Believers above the fray, all three members of the Godhead or Trinity are included in the following scriptures.

Matthew 12:28 "But if I (**Jesus**) cast out demons by the **Spirit of God**, then the **kingdom of God** has come upon you."

Matthew 3:16-17 "After being baptized, **Jesus** came up immediately from the water; and behold, the heavens were opened, and he (Jesus) saw **the Spirit of God** descending as a dove and remaining on Him. And lo, (**GOD**) a voice from Heaven, saying, **this is My beloved Son, in whom I am well pleased.**"

Matthew 28:19 "Go therefore and make disciples of all the nations, baptizing them in the name of **the Father** and **the Son** and **the Holy Spirit** . . ."

Luke 3:22 "And **the Holy Spirit** descended upon Him (**Jesus**) in bodily form like a dove, and a voice came out of heaven, "You are My (**the Father's**) beloved Son, in You I am well-pleased."

John 14:26 "But the Helper, **the Holy Spirit**, whom **the Father** will send **in My (Jesus') name**, He will teach you all things, and bring to your remembrance all that I said to you."

John 15:26 "When the Helper comes, whom **I (Jesus)** will send to you from **the Father**, that is **the Spirit of truth** who proceeds <u>from **the Father**</u>, He will **<u>testify about Me</u>** . . ."

Acts 1:4 "Gathering them together, **He (Jesus)** commanded them not to leave Jerusalem, but to wait for what **the Father** had promised (**<u>the Holy Spirit</u>**), "Which," He said, "**<u>you heard of from Me</u>** . . ."

Acts 2:33 "Therefore having been exalted **to the right hand of God** and <u>having received **from the Father**</u> the **promise of the Holy Spirit, He (Jesus)** has poured forth this which you both see and hear."

Acts 10:38 "You know of **Jesus of Nazareth**, how **God anointed Him** with **the Holy Spirit** and <u>with power</u>, and how <u>He went about doing good and healing all who were oppressed by the devil,</u> **for GOD was with Him.**"

Romans 1:4 "Who was declared **the Son of God** with power by the resurrection from the dead, according **to the Spirit** of holiness, **Jesus Christ our Lord** . . ."

Romans 8:9 "However, you are not in the flesh but in **the Spirit**, if indeed **the Spirit of God dwells in you**. But if anyone does not have **the Spirit of Christ**, he does not belong **to Him**."

1ˢᵗ Corinthians 6:11 Such were some of you; but you were washed, but you were sanctified, but you were justified in the **name of the <u>Lord Jesus Christ</u>** and in <u>**the Spirit**</u> of <u>**our God**</u>.

2ⁿᵈ Corinthians 13:14 The grace of **the Lord Jesus Christ**, and the **love of God**, and **the fellowship of the Holy Spirit**, *be with you all.*

Galatians 4:6 Because <u>you are sons</u>, **God** has sent forth **the Spirit** of **His Son** into our hearts, crying, "Abba! Father!"

Ephesians 1:17 That **the God** of our **Lord Jesus Christ**, the **Father of glory**, may give to you **a spirit of wisdom and of revelation in the knowledge of Him.**

Ephesians 2:18 For through **Him** we both have our access in **one Spirit** to **the Father.**

Ephesians 2:22 **In whom (Jesus)** you also are being built together into a **dwelling of God** in **the Spirit.**

Titus 3:4-7 and when the kindness and the love to men of God our Savior did appear (not by works that *are* in righteousness that we did but according to His kindness,) He did save us, through a bathing of regeneration, and a renewing of **the Holy Spirit**, which **He poured upon us richly**, through **Jesus Christ our Savior**, that having <u>been declared righteous by His grace</u>, heirs we may become according to the hope of life age-during. **Whom (the Holy Spirit) He (GOD) poured out upon us richly through Jesus Christ our Savior.**

Hebrews 9:14 How much more will the **blood of Christ**, who through **the eternal Spirit** offered **Himself without blemish to God**, <u>cleanse your conscience from dead works to serve</u> **<u>the living God</u>**?

1ˢᵗ Peter 1:2 According to the foreknowledge of **God the Father**, by the **sanctifying work of the Spirit**, to obey **Jesus Christ** and be sprinkled with His blood: <u>may grace and peace be yours in the fullest measure.</u>

Of course, there are more passages that mention all three Trinity members of the Godhead (1st Corinthians 12:4–6; Ephesians 1:13–14; 4:4–6; Jude 20–21), and many more that describe the relationships between the three persons of the Godhead or Trinity, but these are enough to declare the Godhead's love for mankind and more for Believers in Jesus Christ to know that everything in this world was created for Believers and nothing was made for <u>unbelievers</u> <u>except</u> <u>salvation</u>. Also, the Godhead wants to bless Believers with good and <u>not punish Believers at all.</u>

The point to listing the scriptures and showing the collaboration of all three aspects of the Godhead working for Believers growth and development **is to introduce life with Jesus, Himself**. Chapter 3 is Jesus <u>in his own words presenting Believers with a new way to "live in Christ and letting Christ live through you"</u>, every day, all the time. Now that Believers have the Bible, it is important to use it, because <u>the word of</u> <u>**GOD is GOD**</u>. If you want to know GOD, get to know GOD's word and the love of GOD, which is <u>the subject line</u> of the entire Bible.

Peter brings good news at Pentecost.

The sermon at Pentecost that produced the Salvation and Baptizing of 3,000 with "GOD, the Holy Spirit" is a picture of the evangelistic approach to Christianity before there was a Bible. Three thousand men were saved and filled with the Holy Spirit after this witness from Peter.

Acts 2:14-21 But Peter, standing up with the Eleven, lifted up his voice and said to them, <u>Men, Jews, and all who dwell at Jerusalem</u>, let this be known to you, and listen to my words. <u>For these are not drunk as you suppose, for it is *the* third hour of the day</u>. But this is that which was spoken by the prophet Joel: "And it shall be in the last days, says God, <u>I will pour out of My Spirit upon all flesh</u>. And your sons and your daughters shall prophesy, and your young men shall see visions, and your old men shall dream dreams. And in those days, <u>I will pour out My Spirit upon</u> My slaves and My slave women, and they shall prophesy. **And I will give <u>wonders in the heaven above, and miracles on the earth below</u>,** blood and fire and vapor of smoke. <u>The sun shall be turned into darkness</u> and <u>the moon into blood</u>, before that great and glorious Day of the Lord. **And it shall be** *that* **everyone who shall call upon the name of the Lord shall be saved.**"

Acts 2:22 Men, Israelites, hear these words. Jesus of Nazareth, a man approved of God among you <u>by powerful works, and wonders, and miracles,</u> **which God did through Him in your midst**, as you yourselves also know, this One given *to you* by the before-determined counsel and foreknowledge of God, <u>*you* have taken and by lawless hands, crucifying *Him*, you put Him to death</u>; **whom God raised up**, having loosed the pains of death, because it was not possible that He should be held by it. For David speaks concerning Him, "I foresaw the Lord always before me, because He is at my right hand, that I should not be moved. Therefore, my heart rejoiced, and my tongue was glad; and also My flesh shall rest in hope, because **You will not leave My soul in Hades, <u>nor will You allow Your holy One to see corruption</u>**. <u>You revealed to Me the ways of life. You will fill Me with joy with Your countenance.</u>"

Acts 2:29 Men, brothers, it is permitted to say to you with plainness as to the patriarch David, that he is both dead and buried, and his tomb is with us to this day. Therefore being a prophet, and knowing that God had sworn with an oath to him that of *the* fruit of his loins, according to the flesh, <u>He would raise up Christ to sit upon his throne</u>, seeing this beforehand, he spoke of the resurrection of Christ, that His soul was not left in

Hades, nor would His flesh see corruption, **God raised up this Jesus, of which we all are witnesses**.

Acts 2:33 Therefore being exalted to the right of God and having received from the Father the promise of the Holy Spirit, He has poured out this which you now see and hear. For David has not ascended into the heavens, but he says himself, "The LORD said to my Lord, Sit at My right *hand* until I place Your enemies *as* a footstool to Your feet." Therefore, let all the house of Israel know assuredly that God made this same Jesus, whom you crucified, both Lord and Christ (Messiah). And hearing *this*, they were stabbed in the heart, and said to Peter and to the other apostles, Men, brothers, what shall we do?

Acts 2:38-41 Then Peter said to them, **Repent and be baptized, every one of you, in the name of Jesus Christ to remission of sins, and you shall receive the gift of the Holy Spirit.** For the promise is to you and to your children, and to all those afar off, as many as *the* Lord our God shall call. And with many other words he earnestly testified and exhorted, saying, be saved from this perverse generation. Then those who gladly received his word were baptized. And the same day there were added about **three thousand souls**.

Wow and now, listen to Peter when he preaches to the Gentiles, that he did not know were to be included in receiving The Messiah, until this experience.

Gentiles Hear the Good News

Acts 10:34-43 So Peter opened his mouth and said: "**Truly I understand that God shows no partiality**, but in every nation (every ethnicity) anyone who fears him and does what is right is acceptable to him. As for the word that he sent to Israel, preaching good news of peace **through Jesus Christ** (he is

Lord of <u>all</u>), you yourselves know what happened throughout all Judea, beginning from Galilee after the baptism that John proclaimed: **how God anointed Jesus of Nazareth with the Holy Spirit and with power.** <u>He went about doing good and</u> **<u>healing all who were oppressed by the devil, for God was</u>** <u>with him</u>. <u>And we are witnesses of all that he did both in the country of the Jews and in Jerusalem.</u> They put him to death by hanging him on a tree, **but God raised him on the third day and made him to appear,** not to all the people but to us who had been chosen by God as witnesses, who ate and drank with him after he rose from the dead. <u>And he commanded us to preach to the people and to testify that he is the one appointed by God to be judge of the living and the dead.</u> To him all the prophets bear witness that <u>everyone who believes in him receives forgiveness of sins through his name.</u>"

The Holy Spirit Falls on the Gentiles

Acts 10:44-48 While Peter was still speaking these words, **the Holy Spirit fell on all those hearing the Word.** And those of the circumcision (Jews), who believed (as many as came with Peter), were astonished **because the gift of the Holy Spirit was poured out on the nations (other ethnicities)** also. <u>For they heard them speak with tongues and magnify God.</u> Then **Peter answered, can anyone forbid water that these, who have received the Holy Ghost as well as we,** should not be baptized? And he commanded them to be baptized in the name of the Lord (in water). Then they begged him to stay certain days.

The GOSPEL is the coming of the Messiah, the reversing of the penalty of <u>sin, sickness, oppression, and separation from GOD</u>. To Believers, Jesus returned the authority to reign on earth, <u>Jesus restored GOD's glory to Believers</u>, and gave the gift of "GOD, the Holy Spirit" to live inside Believers and be on Believers. And all this, so Believers could give GOD's love to their family, their neighbor, and to the world, and be seen as "the praise" of GOD's glory.

Chapter 2

Your Death Certificate, Your Birth Certificate.
Your new Passport, Your new ID.

When did you receive your Spiritual Birth Certificate for the Kingdom of GOD on earth? It is good to know when you received Jesus Christ into your heart and started living for Him, but if you don't have a specific day, lets claim today (you can add a year date later when you think about the timing) but today is your day for your adult starting point for faith in Jesus, as Savior and GOD, the Holy Spirit as your seal into the Family of GOD.

Many Believers do not understand that Jesus died for the sins of all mankind, when Jesus went to the cross and was resurrected, the sacrifice included everyone who had ever lived or would live. Everyone who has ever lived or will live has no penalty owing in their sin account **but only Believers who have chosen Jesus and had Jesus put his righteousness in the Believers account are reconciled to GOD**. Whatever GOD, does, is done for all and for all time because GOD is Truth and in Him there is no variance. Remember, at one time we were all unbelievers. It is mankind's free-will to choose **Jesus as Savior**, that separates mankind into two groups: Believers and unbelievers. Listen to the explanation from the Apostle Paul.

Romans 6:4-8 Therefore we were buried with Him by baptism into death, so that as Christ was raised up from *the* dead by the glory of the Father; even so we also should walk in newness of life. For if we have been joined together in the likeness of His death, **we shall also be *in the likeness* of His resurrection**; knowing this, that our old man is crucified with *Him* in order that **the body of sin might be destroyed**, that from now on <u>we should not serve sin</u>. For he who died has been justified from sin. <u>But if we died with Christ, we believe that we shall also</u> **live with Him,**

Step 1; The Lord's death **paid the penalty** for the <u>universe of sin</u>.

Step 2; "Belief in" and choosing the Lord, <u>as Savior</u>, exchanges the Believers "nature to sin" for the Lord's "Nature of GOD" through His righteousness. Now, eternal life and **right-standing** <u>with GOD are yours</u>. It is the Born-again experience that offers a <u>Death Certificate</u> to the family of Adam and Eve and a **Birth Certificate** <u>to the Kingdom of GOD's dear Son; Jesus your Spiritual Father.</u>

**Our new Spirit came from Jesus,
And Jesus Christ is in Believers
as "GOD, the Holy Spirit".**

One of the greatest facts of the Christian faith is the amazing truth that the Lord Jesus Christ indwells each believer through sending "GOD, the Holy Spirit". The Apostle Paul said, "Christ lives in me,"

Galatians 2:20 I am crucified with Christ: nevertheless I live; **yet not I, but Christ lives in me**: and <u>the life which I now live in the flesh</u> I live **by the <u>faith of</u> the Son of God**, who loved me, and gave himself for me. KJV

Many Bibles say, "I now live by faith "in" the Son of GOD", but the context of the New Testament is to believe on an event that happened 1995 years ago and translate or appropriate a gift of grace that was manifested by the Lord's faith into your heart.

And NOW to appropriate the gift from Jesus, the Apostle Paul wants Believers to believe in the Lord's faith, and <u>die</u> **to ourselves <u>with Him</u>** and <u>to</u> **be raised with Him** <u>in his resurrection</u>, so **that Jesus can live in us**. NOW, **have faith in the Lord's faith**, that **it is not you living**, but **Jesus is living in you**. Let us break this down in the first person for you. Say this with me.

- Jesus had faith for my Salvation through his dying and receiving the punishment for my sins.
- Jesus had faith for my healing by taking the scourging in his body and suffering the pain of sickness.
- Jesus had faith for my iniquity by taking the bruising in his body and suffering the pain of iniquity.
- Jesus had faith for living the "Old Law" to the letter so that I do not receive the curses for my inability to live the law to the letter, for cursed is him who is hanged on a tree.
- **Father GOD sees me as saved, healed, delivered, sanctified, redeemed from all curses, and blessed with all the blessings GOD gave to Abraham.**

Have faith in what Jesus has done, <u>not faith in your action, it is Christ living in you that gives you the collaboration to save, heal, or deliver GOD's children in need.</u> Think about this, **are you trying to receive something that is already a fact**?

<u>Think about this prayer:</u> **Father GOD you already believe** that I am saved, healed, delivered, and blessed by the finished works of Jesus, my heart is full of thanksgiving for all that you have done for me, <u>help my unbelief.</u>

This prayer is truly a picture of the GOD kind of love, and pumps up the Believer's called to represent Christ with our lives as Ambassadors to the Kingdom of GOD on earth.

- Your Identification with Adam is dead, **your old self was crucified with Jesus** and your New Spirit is raised with **the resurrection of Jesus.**
- Your new ID is with Jesus Christ and **the new you** lives because **you were raised in Newness of life** with Jesus at His resurrection.
- Jesus has given you "GOD, the Holy Spirit" to be one with your Spirit and is the Believer's Passport to the Life with Christ.

Your new ID and Spirit are brand new. You now have a death certificate for your old self or "sin nature" and a Birth Certificate for entrance into the Kingdom of GOD's dear Son and a Passport to travel with "GOD, the Holy Spirit" through Eternal Life with Christ.

Hallelujah, Hallelujah!

How did Father GOD orchestrate this transformation?

Everything in GOD's Kingdom reproduces after its seed: the fruit, flower, vegetable, animal, fish, or human has the seed inside themselves for the next generation whether human, plant, or animal. The seed of everything, is in the male side. Adam and Eve were the master copies of mankind, made in the exact image of GOD, until Adam broke covenant with GOD and corrupted their seed. Now everyone born of the seed of Adam was and is born with a dead spirit or malware in their DNA or born with a "nature to sin" instead of the "Spirit of GOD".

When Father GOD sent His word and encompassed Mary, <u>the seed of His word impregnated Mary</u> and Jesus was born of incorruptible seed. NOW, everyone who is Born-again, into the Kingdom of GOD, <u>is born from an incorruptible seed and is given a Spirit made in the Image of GOD</u> and is a child of GOD. **The Spirit part of a Believer is made perfect by Jesus and that Spirit can fellowship with GOD.**

GOD had to plant a new seed into mankind to restore a Godly line of children born-again from this new seed of the Spirit of GOD. The seed of GOD's word in Jesus Christ has given new life to mankind, who receive the seed and are "Born-again".

For Jesus to redeem mankind and reconcile mankind to GOD, Jesus had to be born a man, born of woman, from the seed of GOD's word. Jesus Christ is the Word of GOD made flesh with the nature of GOD in his Spirit. **The seed from GOD's word made flesh, has restored mankind's power over everything on the earth, above the earth, and below the earth through their "New Spirit" and the gift of "GOD, the Holy Spirit".** "GOD, the Holy Spirit" is inside Believers right now. Listen to the Apostle Paul describe this transformation.

Colossians 1:9-14 <u>For this cause</u> we also, since the day we heard, do not cease to pray for you, and to desire that you might <u>be filled *with* the knowledge of His will in all wisdom and spiritual understanding,</u> that you might walk worthy of the Lord to all pleasing, being fruitful in every work and increasing in the knowledge of God, **being empowered with all power,** according to the might of His glory, to **all patience and long-suffering with joyfulness,** giving thanks to the Father, <u>who has made us meet to be partakers of the inheritance of the saints in light.</u> *For He* has delivered us <u>from</u> the power of darkness and has translated *us* into **the kingdom of His dear Son**; in whom we have redemption through His blood, the remission of sins.

Think about the Lord's prayer, "Thy Kingdom come", it does not say, "Believers will go". **The Kingdom of our King, Jesus Christ has come**. Then Father GOD sent HIS Holy Spirit to inhabit the Spiritual Kingdom in every Believer's New heart or Spirit on earth. Listen to the words of Jesus.

John 16:13-15 When the Spirit of truth comes, he will guide you into all the truth, (Jesus is Grace and truth) for he will not speak on his own authority, but whatever he hears he will speak, and he will declare to you **the things that are to come**. He will glorify me, for he will take what is mine and declare it to you. **All that the Father has is mine**; therefore, I said that **he will take what is mine and declare it to you.**

Meditate on this scripture and the guiding of the Holy Spirit for your life with "GOD, the Holy Spirit " inside your new Spirit living Spirit to Spirit with you. You are never alone, ever again, Jesus said, I will never leave you nor forsake you. So, the question is, "Do you believe GOD?"

Listen to the Apostle Paul give us some additional details about what your new ID is and how it happened. Believers are now part of the body of Jesus Christ which is the Church, the Bride of Jesus.

Colossians 1:21-28 And you, who were once alienated and enemies in *your* mind by wicked works, yet now Jesus has reconciled in the body of His flesh through death, to present you holy and without blemish, and without charge in His sight,

if indeed you continue in the faith grounded and settled, and *are* not moved away from the hope of the gospel, which you have heard *and* which was proclaimed in all the creation under Heaven, of which I, Paul, became a minister, who now rejoice in my sufferings on your behalf, and I fill up the things lacking of the afflictions of Christ in my flesh, on behalf of His body, which *is* the church; of which I became a minister, according to the administration of God given to me <u>for you</u>, to fulfill the Word of God;

the mystery which has been hidden from ages and from generations, but now has been revealed to His saints. *For to them* God would make known what *are* the riches of the glory of this mystery among the (races) nations, <u>which is Christ in you, the hope of glory,</u> whom we preach, warning every man and teaching every man in all wisdom, **so that we may present every man perfect in Christ Jesus to GOD.**

Notice, <u>the mystery was Christ in you, the Hope of Glory,</u> and <u>Christ is in you</u> **to present you perfect to Father GOD**. The Believers Spirit is perfect and is sealed and cannot be penetrated by <u>the Believers lawless acts or thoughts</u> **but is mighty when united with the purpose of Christ in you**. The purpose and authority of your Passport from Jesus is to <u>fill the world with your witness of the love of GOD and to build the Church of Jesus Christ</u>. Listen to part of the Apostle Paul's calling to preach "Jesus living in Paul" to the nations.

Galatians 1:15-16 But when it pleased God, who separated me from my mother's womb, and having called *me* by His grace, <u>to reveal His Son "in me"</u> so that I might preach Him among the nations, immediately I did <u>not</u> confer with flesh and blood;

Notice, <u>all Believers have been called to reveal the Son of GOD</u> **in them** <u>that we may be a witness</u> among the nations or races. And this revelation is not from flesh and blood but from the

Believer's New Spirit made in the exact image of GOD by our Savior Jesus Christ.

What was the Starting point
for your Birth Certificate and Death Certificate?
When did you really know you believed GOD?

Believers must have a Birth Certificate to prove citizenship for entry into the Kingdom of GOD's dear Son and a Death Certificate for your old nature. Think about this, when you came to the border crossing as an alien and asked for asylum into the Kingdom of GOD's dear Son, was it then, you realized that you needed a Death Certificate from the kingdom of sin and selfishness and a Birth Certificate for entry into the Kingdom of GOD? There is no dual citizenship in the Kingdom of GOD. The requirements for a Passport to travel in the Kingdom of GOD in the Seen world and in the Spirit, is belief in "GOD, the Holy Spirit" and in who sent Him?

You may be asking "how do I get a passport for the Kingdom of GOD, "How do I know where I stand with GOD?" "Is there a scale to measure my life?" and "How good do I have to be?" "Is it, I will do my best and Jesus will make-up the rest, is that in the Bible somewhere?" NO, NO, NO.

You must be Born-again into the Kingdom of Jesus Christ to get a Birth Certificate <u>into the Kingdom of GOD</u>, Citizenship is all about <u>where you were born and **who is King**</u>.

Listen to the Apostle Paul describe the process.

Romans 6:3-5 Do you <u>not</u> know that all of us who have been baptized into Christ Jesus were baptized into his death? We were buried therefore with him by baptism into death, in order that, <u>just as Christ was raised from the dead by the glory of the Father</u>, **we too might walk in newness of life. For if we have been united with him in <u>a death like his</u>, we shall certainly be united with him in a resurrection like his.**

In History, before there was an earthly Kingdom of GOD's dear Son, what did people do? How did Abraham get his passport into GOD's Kingdom?

Genesis 15:6 And Abraham believed the LORD, and <u>GOD counted it to him as righteousness.</u>

Abraham trusted <u>that GOD **could do what He promised**</u> and GOD granted his "belief" as righteousness. **What if "Belief" is the <u>starting point</u> for all relationships with GOD and "trust-in GOD" <u>the second step?</u>**

How did the Hebrew nation receive a passport out of Egypt and slavery? What is the "belief progression" at the first Passover in Egypt. A beaten down people (descendants of Jacob) who had been in slavery for over four-hundred years **believed** when GOD said, **"trust me"** <u>kill and eat a lamb and put the blood of the lamb on the lentil and the door posts of your dwelling and then the death angel will pass-over your family and you will leave slavery and Egypt tomorrow, rich and without a feeble one among you.</u>

Israel after coming through the Red Sea on dry land and watching the Egyptian army drown in the sea they had just crossed, soon arrived at Mt Sinai. FIRST, GOD announced, He has given the Israelites inclusion into His family when He said, **"You are My people and I am your GOD"**, without condition. Israel did not receive the law as a way to get to GOD, but the law was designed to develop a new culture for a people who had been in slavery for four hundred years.

**GOD made a way for all to join His Family,
FIRST.**

We need to put into practice what Jesus told His disciples, "Deny yourself (your old nature), take up your cross (your new nature), and follow Me". What is taking up our cross daily?

We need to die to our own goals, our own agenda, and our own desires to properly serve Christ, <u>by loving others as Christ has loved us.</u> Remember, Believers have been sent into the world as Jesus was sent into the world, to turn the world right side up. Believers must **<u>not</u>** be motivated by selfish desires but be engulfed by the love of GOD for all people. GOD has promised to give Believers a new set of desires. (*Psalms 37:3-4*)

In the New Testament the Apostle Paul explains this idea of love, service, and worship taken to a new level, "A living sacrifice".

Romans 12:1-2 I appeal to you therefore, brothers, by the mercies of God, to present your bodies as a living sacrifice, <u>holy and acceptable to God</u>, which is your spiritual worship. Do not be conformed to this world, <u>but</u> be <u>transformed by the renewal of your mind</u>, that by testing you may discern what is the will of God, what is <u>good</u> and <u>acceptable</u> and <u>perfect</u>.

The question for every Believer is do you believe GOD; The Messiah has come, the Bible is true, GOD can deliver everything GOD has promised? What is the basis and focus of your life?

**The Lord's sacrifice,
gives way to our New Life.**

Today, we do not have any eyewitnesses to the resurrection to jumpstart our adult faith in Jesus Christ, but Believers today are blessed to have **The Bible,** inspired by GOD, and recorded by eyewitnesses to the events and words of Jesus Christ. John 14,15,16,17, and Romans 8 details how God has graced Believers, by indwelling Believers with "GOD, the Holy Spirit" so we can be empowered to <u>live right</u> by <u>believing GOD and His Word.</u>

Romans 8:9-11 You, however, are not in the flesh but in the Spirit, **if in fact the Spirit of God dwells in you**. Anyone who does not have the Spirit of Christ does not belong to him. But if Christ is in you, although the body is dead because of sin, <u>the Spirit is life</u> **because of righteousness**. If the Spirit of him who raised Jesus from the dead **dwells in you**, he who raised Christ Jesus from the dead <u>will also give life to your mortal bodies through his Spirit who dwells in you.</u>

This description of the indwelling of GOD in Believers is inspiring and eye opening. What fabulous news for everyone who is dwelling "One with **GOD, the Holy Spirit**" inside every Believer.

**GOD's plan for the earth and mankind
was and will be great again.**

Adam, Eve, and Jesus were created and born perfect representations of GOD, they started life filled 100% with the "Nature of GOD", the exact image and likeness of GOD. There was **<u>no</u>** appreciable difference in the lives of Adam and Eve, and Jesus until Adam and Eve broke covenant with Father GOD. There was an automatic consequence for breaking covenant; the introduction of <u>Spiritual death,</u> introduction <u>of evil,</u> and <u>physical perishing</u> that automatically started because of their rebellion.

If forgiveness could have been a remedy for Adam and Eve breaking covenant with GOD, <u>GOD could have forgiven Adam, Eve, and Lucifer with His mercy</u>, but **The Consequences for disobedience required redemption, <u>not</u> <u>forgiveness</u>**. Remember, GOD is faithful and just <u>at the same time</u>. Jesus Christ received the Believers punishment for sin and the covenant breaking of Adam and Eve and suffered the wrath of GOD for all sin. And GOD was faithful to give Believers a new Spirit and Covenant with GOD for everyone Born-again.

Think about this:

Mankind was created with the Nature of GOD, .

made in the exact image of GOD, without death.

In the beginning, living <u>without the law</u> to transgress,

living without a conscious of failure,

living life **filled with love**,

and the "Fruit of the Spirit" of GOD.

Choosing Father God for who GOD is.

That choice was Father GOD's plan A.

Adam and Eve choosing <u>with their free-will</u>

to break Covenant with GOD, <u>was not GOD's hope,</u>

reconciling mankind into a new Covenant with GOD

Through Jesus is GOD's Plan B.

Mankind has a choice,

life with Christ Jesus

or death by rejecting the sacrifice of Jesus.

GOD hopes you choose Life. **But it is your choice**.

GOD's plan B required sending Jesus to live as a man, with a free-will to choose, to die to redeem mankind for the mess Adam, Eve, and Lucifer started. GOD could **not** forgive mankind for breaking covenant with GOD, because of GOD's word in the Covenant agreement that contained an automatic consequence. Redemption must come from another word from GOD, and that word was made flesh and became the second Adam, Jesus Christ filled with the "Nature of GOD".

Jesus was, "a new seed from the word of GOD", made flesh, a man filled 100% with the Nature of GOD and without one sin, who chose to love GOD and mankind, and give his life to redeem Mankind and receive the wrath of GOD for the sin of the universe. GOD has now offered right-standing (reconciliation to GOD) to anyone who believes in Jesus Christ **and Father GOD, who sent Him**. Just as Abraham believed GOD and it was accounted to him as righteousness, so every Believer born-again from the "New Seed" of Jesus Christ has believed and is in right standing with GOD.

Think about the picture we have of Abraham sacrificing Isaac, where we see the first use of the word "worship" and "love" in the Bible. Genesis 22:2-5.

Genesis 22:2 And He said, take now your son, your only one, Isaac, **whom you love**. And go into the land of Moriah and <u>offer him there for a burnt offering</u> upon one of the mountains which I will name to you.

Genesis 22:5 And Abraham said unto his young men, abide ye here with the ass; and I and the lad will go yonder and **<u>worship</u>**, and come again to you. Vs. 22:16…. <u>declares the LORD</u>, because you have done this and have not withheld your son, your only son, I will surely bless you, and I will surely multiply your offspring as the stars of heaven and as the sand that is on the seashore. And your offspring shall possess the gate of his enemies, and in your offspring shall all the nations (ethnicities or races) of the earth be blessed, because you have obeyed my voice.

This devotion to GOD is a preview of what the Lord did for mankind, and what Jesus asked us to do when Jesus said, "If anyone would come after me, let him deny himself and take up his cross and follow me. For whoever would save his life will lose it, but whoever loses his life <u>for my sake</u> will find it." Matthew 16:24-25.

Most people think of themselves as serving God, but they do it based on their terms and their timing. They compartmentalize God and make Worship "only on Sunday" or only when they are <u>not</u> serving themselves.

How do we picture GOD?
If your picture of GOD is flawed
your decisions will be flawed.

Think about these three reactions to problems in our daily life in a fallen world.

1. Believers turn to GOD when something bad happens, but we believe that if GOD had been there, GOD would have prevented what happened.

We assume facts not in evidence, we assume GOD allowed the calamity that happened, which is in direct opposition to GOD's promise to give mankind dominion on the earth.

James 1:13 Let no one <u>being tempted</u> say, I am tempted from God. For God is not tempted by evils, and <u>He tempts no one.</u>

Now a second misconception about thoughts about GOD.

2. After you believe that GOD allowed a calamity to happen, then it does not matter if GOD intervenes, to help due to reaching out to GOD with prayer or using His promises, because we have already judged that GOD was not there when the calamity happened.

Again, we assume facts not in evidence, <u>GOD is all powerful,</u> **but has restricted His power by the free-will choices of Mankind**. If you believe GOD caused or allowed a calamity, then **why should you pray for something GOD did or allowed?**

Now a third misconception about thoughts about GOD.

3. If there is no positive answer from GOD to the prayer for deliverance or a miracle for the calamity, then the people praying are sure that there is something separating them from GOD.

Again, we assume facts not in evidence, there is nothing that can separate a Believer from the love of GOD. Listen to the Apostle Paul.

<u>*Romans 8:37-39*</u> But in all these things we more than conquer through **Him who loved us**. For I am persuaded **that neither death, nor life, nor angels, nor principalities, nor powers, nor things present, nor things to come, nor height, nor depth, nor any other creature, shall be able to separate us from the love of God which is in Christ Jesus our Lord.**

Until Believers have **knowledge of the authority of mankind on earth** and <u>the power of GOD's word inside Believers</u> their incorrect thinking used in these three examples keep Believers in bondage to <u>bad thinking</u>. **GOD's view of Believers is the perfection of His son**. Jesus absorbed all of GOD's wrath for the penalty of "All sin", past, present, and future. Believers should be living in no condemnation, freed from all sin.

Chapter 3

Jesus announces a NEW way of life,
Not just believing but following Jesus and
Embracing "GOD, the Holy Spirit".

Listen to Jesus, telling Believers His plan for our lives, after your Born-again experience. The new systems for operating in the Church age with Jesus Christ and "GOD, the Holy Spirit" <u>are hidden in plain sight</u>. These NEW ways of living, **reverse** the current system of <u>reacting to the situations of life in man-made power</u>, **to controlling the issues of life from inside your being where you and your GOD are ONE**. Each one of these statements appear in the New Testament and most are said by Jesus Christ.

Believers are a new creation in our Spirit.

Believers have a new way to Father GOD.

Believers have a new world in the Spirit with "GOD, the Holy Spirit".

Believers have a new High Priest.

Believers have a new and living way of life.

Believers have a new way to pray.

Believers have a new commandment to rule their life.

Believers are part of a new Covenant.

Believers have a new inheritance from Jesus Christ.

Believers are New Men and Women living in and through Jesus Christ.

Believers hear the voice of **the Lord**, <u>know Him, and follow Him.</u>

Now read the confirmations of the Lord's plan for Believer's lives, from Jesus own words or inspiration, written in the New Testament. Each promise or description is **not** how to live in the Believers own power, but **how to be "One with GOD" and let Jesus live in Believers.**

- **<u>A New Creation in Believers</u>**.

The Spiritual part of every Believer is <u>new,</u> and **your new Spirit is a perfect representation of GOD**, <u>made in the image and likeness of GOD</u>. Your New Spirit is freed from sin having been made perfect by Jesus Christ. Any Believers sin from bad habits is not counted against GOD's new creation.

2nd Corinthians 5:16-19 So as we **now** know "<u>no one</u>" <u>according to flesh</u>, but even if we have known Christ according to flesh, yet now we no longer know *Him so*. So that <u>if anyone is</u> in Christ, ***that one is* a new creature**; old things (sin nature) have passed away; behold, (the Born-again Spirit) <u>all things have become new</u>. And <u>all things *are* of God</u>, who has reconciled us <u>(Believers) to Himself</u> through Jesus Christ, and has given to us the ministry of reconciliation, whereas God was in Christ reconciling *the* world to Himself, **not** imputing (counting) their trespasses to them, and <u>putting the word of reconciliation in us.</u>

<u>Context for "A New Creation in Believers"</u>; One third of a Believer's being, "Your Born-again Spirit" is <u>New</u> and <u>perfect</u> because it is created from the incorruptible seed of GOD's word made flesh Jesus Christ. Now Believers should no longer look at others according to what they look like, or sound like, or where they live, or what church they attend, but **now Believers**

look at everyone as a creation of GOD and it is our destiny to treat everyone the way Jesus treated everyone.

- ### A New way to the Father.

The Lord Jesus Christ is the all-sufficient way, the new way, and the perfect way, to Father God. It is not that <u>He shows the way</u>; <u>He is the way</u>, Jesus is alive, and all who want to come to The Father must come to God through Him. Believers can talk to GOD all day because, Jesus died to open the communication channel with GOD and Believer.

Jesus said, I Am the Way, the Truth, and <u>the Life</u>. *John 14:6*

Do you not know that **<u>Believers are a temple of God</u>**, and *that* **the Spirit of God dwells in you**? *1st Corinthians 3:16*

For to them God would make known what *are* the riches of **the glory of this mystery** among the nations, **which is Christ in <u>you</u>**, <u>the hope of glory</u>, *Colossians 1:27*

Heaven will be heavenly, but GOD made the earth to fellowship with Believers. Many churches do not teach about the gift of "GOD the Holy Spirit" being inside Believers on earth but, GOD cares about the Believers life on earth it is here that the promises of GOD give Believers the abundant life. Heaven will happen automatically as a part of eternal life but the treasure you store up in Heaven comes from your time on earth and is very important.

These next verses emphasize living in and through the Spirit of GOD, focused on the plan of GOD, loving others as Jesus has loved mankind.

Psalms 91:1-2 He that dwelleth in the secret place of the most High shall abide under the shadow of the Almighty. I will say of the LORD, *He is* my refuge and my fortress: my God; <u>in him will I trust.</u>

Psalms 91:9-10 Because Believers have made the LORD, *which is* my refuge, *even* <u>the most High, my habitation;</u> There shall no evil befall you, neither shall any plague come nigh <u>your dwelling.</u>

John 15:5-7 I am the Vine, you *are* the branches. He who abides in Me, and I in him, the same brings forth much fruit; for without Me you can do nothing. <u>If anyone does not abide in Me, he is cast out as a branch and is withered. And they gather and cast *them* into the fire, and they are burned.</u> **If you abide in Me, and My Words abide in you, you shall ask what you will, and it shall be done to you.**

When you dwell in the secret place of the Most High, when the Most High is your refuge, when you abide in GOD and Jesus abides in you, ask what you will for you have found your Father and you are in the Family of GOD.

<u>Think about these scriptures and the ones following and judge for yourself, Jesus has given Believers a new way to live with Jesus living though Believers.</u>

- **Father GOD sends <u>"GOD, the Holy Spirit"</u> to be with Believers forever.**

John 14:15-21 "If you love me, you will keep my (instructions) commandments. And I will ask the Father, and **the Father will give you another Helper,** <u>to be with you forever,</u> even the Spirit of truth, whom the world cannot receive, because it neither sees him nor knows him.

You know him, for **he dwells with you** and **will be in you.**

I will not leave you as orphans.

I will come to you. Yet a little while and

the world will see me no more,

but you will see me.

Because I live, you also will live.

In that day **you will know**

that **I am in my Father,**

and you in me, and I in you.

Whoever has my commandments and keeps them,

he it is who loves me. And he who loves me

will be loved by my Father, and

I will love him

and manifest myself to him."

"Lord, how is it that you will manifest yourself to us,

and not to the world?"

"If anyone loves me, he will keep my word

And **my Father will love him,**

and **we will come to him**

and make our home with him.

Context and the giving of "GOD, the Holy Spirit" to Believers.
If you believe "GOD, the Holy Spirit" is inside you for

leadership, comfort, and power; **nothing is impossible when you are "One with GOD".** Talk to "GOD, the Holy Spirit" until you can hear his voice talking back in your mind. Study the New Testament to know the language of "GOD, the Holy Spirit". Allow the peace of GOD to rule in your heart to govern your actions. If your heart is not at peace with your thoughts and actions **stop and re-align yourself with GOD**.

- **Jesus is our New High Priest from the High Priestly order of Melchizedek.**

Jesus is the New High Priest and mediator of a New and Better Covenant developed on better promises.

Hebrews 8:6-9 But now **Jesus has obtained a more excellent *new* ministry,** by so much He is also **the Mediator *of a New and* better covenant, which was built upon better promises**. For if that first *covenant* had been without fault, *then* no place would have been sought for *the* second. **For finding fault with them**, He said to them, "**Behold**, days are coming, says *the* Lord, and **I will** make an end on the house of Israel and on the house of Judah (Gentiles); a new covenant ***shall be***, not according to the covenant that I made with their fathers in the day I took hold of their hand to lead them out of the land of Egypt," because they did not continue in My covenant, and I did not regard them, says the Lord.

Hebrews 4:14-16 Since then we have a **great high priest** who has passed through the heavens, **Jesus, the Son of God**, let us hold fast our confession. For we do not have a high priest who is unable to sympathize with our weaknesses, but one who in every respect **has been tempted as we are**, yet without sin. Let us then with confidence **draw near to the throne of grace**, that we may receive mercy and find grace **to help in time of need**.

<u>**Context** and new fact from Jesus</u>: <u>The Devil is no longer in the presence of GOD accusing the Believers</u>, **Jesus is at GOD's right hand** as our High Priest and the mediator of a new covenant with better promises. "GOD, the Holy Spirit" has been sent to every Believer because the wall of separation has been broken down separating Believers and Father GOD. Believers should fellowship with GOD all day every day, it will change your life and your day. Remember the Apostle Paul's key to living was to let Christ live through you.

- **<u>The New and Living way</u> to the presence of GOD.**

Hebrews 10:19-22 **Therefore, brothers, <u>having boldness to enter into the</u> *Holy of* <u>Holies by the blood of Jesus</u>, <u>by a new and living way</u> which He (Jesus) has consecrated <u>for us</u> through the veil, that is to say, His flesh**; and *having* a High Priest over the house of God, let <u>us draw near</u> with a true heart <u>in full assurance</u> of faith, having our hearts sprinkled from an evil conscience and *our* <u>bodies having been washed with pure water</u>.

You <u>yourselves are our letter of recommendation</u>, **written on our hearts, to be known and read by all**. And you show that **you are a letter from Christ** delivered by us, written not with ink **but with the Spirit of the living God**, not on tablets of stone **but on tablets of human hearts**. <u>Such is the confidence</u> that we have through Christ toward God. Not <u>that we are sufficient in ourselves to claim anything as coming from us</u>, but **our sufficiency is from God**, <u>who has made us</u> **sufficient to be ministers of a new covenant**, not of the letter <u>but of the Spirit</u>.

For the letter kills, **but the Spirit gives life**. Now if the ministry of death, carved in letters on stone, <u>came with such glory</u> that the Israelites could not gaze at Moses' face because of its glory, which was being ended, will not the ministry of the Spirit have even **more glory**? For if there was glory in the ministry of condemnation, <u>the ministry of righteousness must far exceed it in glory</u>. 2nd Corinthians 3:2-9

<u>**Context** and fact of **the New and Living way** to the presence of GOD</u>: Believers now have access to the very presence of GOD to build an intimate "living" relationship with Almighty GOD. **Throw away your consciousness of sin** and <u>accept the gift of Jesus</u> and enter a "living" relationship with GOD **built on love**, <u>not built on the Believer's worthiness</u>, but built on the **worthiness of our Lord**.

To enter a "**New and Living Way**" Believers must **keep our minds on things of the Spirit** and <u>**not**</u> on <u>the problems of earth</u>, for the things on earth are temporary but the things of the Spirit are eternal. Love, joy, peace, goodness, gentleness, faith, longsuffering, meekness, and temperance <u>are the eternal things of the Spirit in every Believer</u>. You own the "Fruit of your Spirit", and they are available for you to call on in all life situations. They are also a reminder of the things of the Spirit to thank GOD for each day, for they are Spirit and Life; the love of Father GOD, the joy of life with Father GOD, the peace that Jesus has given, the goodness that has replaced the selfishness, the gentleness that has replaced the "My Way", the faith of Jesus Christ for the finished works of Believer's inheritance, and more.

- <u>**A new way to pray**</u>**. Another teaching after the Last Supper.**

Jesus taught the Disciples the Model or the Lord's prayer, but it <u>did not include</u> "**the power in the name of Jesus**" because

Jesus had not gone to the cross and been resurrected. **And NOW in this new day**, Jesus gave all Believers a new way to pray.

John 16:20-24 Verily, verily, I say unto you, That you shall weep and lament (at my death), but the world shall rejoice: and you shall be sorrowful (at my crucifixion), but your sorrow shall be turned into joy (at my resurrection).… And you now therefore have sorrow: but I will see you again, and your heart shall rejoice, and your joy, no man takes from you.

And in that day (after the cross) you shall ask "me" nothing. Verily, verily, I say unto you, **Whatsoever ye shall ask the Father in my name, he will give *it* you**. Until now you asked nothing in my name: ask, and you shall receive, **that your joy may be full**.

Context and fact of **the "New Way to Pray from Jesus"**: And in that day when I ascend to the Father you shall ask the Father anything **in my name that will make your joy full**, and **the Father will do it**. *What a promise*. Everything Jesus died to appropriate for Believers is "already done" and available through faith in His promises and in the "Fruit of your Spirit". When a Believer knows and uses the Lord's promises, the promises are letting Christ live through them and when the Believer stands in the stead of Jesus and uses His name, the Father will honor that stand.

- **A New Commandment.** This new commandment replaces all commandments but does not disturb the value of the Ten Commandments given to the Israelites.

John 13:34-36 **A new commandment I give unto you,** That you love one another; as I have loved you, that you also love one another. By this shall all *men* know that you are my disciples, **if you have love one to another.** Simon Peter said to Him, Lord, where do You go? Jesus answered him, Where I go (to the cross) you cannot now follow Me, but you shall follow Me afterward.

Context and fact of the New Commandment from Jesus: Think about "a world" where we love our fellow man or woman, friend or foe, neighbor or enemy, the same way that Jesus loves each Believer and unbeliever. This does not mean that Believers are **not** supposed to stand for right and against wrong. **Remember** GOD is all goodness and all justice. So, it is incumbent on each Believer to be motivated by love for everyone involved in our daily personal activities and **do not judge others**, for judging is way above our paygrade. Study the answers Jesus gave to the Pharisees and other wrongdoers to understand how to treat hateful people with a loving and instructive touch. The Believers' main destiny is to be a witness to the love we have received from our Lord for the people of the world.

Peter could not follow Jesus to the cross but after the cross Peter could follow Jesus through abiding in Him and in His words. **This word from the Lord "Follow me" is meant for all Believers for our time on earth. Give of yourself as I have given you.** (John 13:34-36) Listen to Jesus tell Believers where to live our lives.

John 15:4-7 **Abide in Me, and I in you.** As the branch cannot bear fruit of itself unless it remains in the vine, so neither *can* you unless you **abide in Me.** I am the Vine, you *are* the branches. **He who abides in Me, and I in him,** the same brings forth much fruit; for without Me you can do nothing. If anyone does **not** abide in Me, **he is cast out** as a branch and is withered.

And they gather and cast *them* into the fire, and they are burned. **If you abide in Me, and My Words abide in you, you shall ask what you will, and it shall be done to you**.

Notice, "Life" is being consumed by love and <u>love allows Believers</u> to live in Christ (the Anointing) constantly treating others more significantly than ourselves. If you are rebuked by the hateful, shake the insult off and go to the next person with a need. You have planted a seed in the hateful even if you do not get a chance to water the seed of the word of GOD you planted.

- **<u>A New Covenant. GOD speaking His 5 "I will" statements</u>.**

GOD is re-enforcing the fact that Father GOD included mankind into His family, **first**, by giving a sacrifice for the sin of the entire world, the choice to enter GOD's family is now mankind's.

Hebrews 8:10-13 For this *is* <u>the (New) covenant</u> that **I will** make with the house of Israel after those days, saith the Lord; **I will** <u>put my laws into their mind, and write them in their hearts</u>: and **I will** <u>be to them a God</u>, and they shall be to me a people: And they shall not teach every man his neighbor, and every man his brother, saying, Know the Lord: **for all** shall know me, from the least to the greatest. <u>For **I will**</u> be merciful to their unrighteousness, and their <u>sins</u> and their <u>iniquities</u> **I will remember no more**. In that he saith, <u>A new *covenant*,</u> he hath made the first old. Now that which decays and is old *is* ready to vanish away.

<u>**Context**</u> and A New Covenant from GOD: Life through the Spirit of Jesus Christ is life in the New Covenant. GOD gives you **a new heart, new desires**, a **new destiny**, and <u>**a new Spirit**</u>

made in the image of GOD that can**not** be penetrated with sin. Your body or soul may cause some untoward acts and thoughts, but acts <u>will not change your position with GOD</u>. The untoward acts do carry their own inherent penalty, because they are <u>not</u> blessed by GOD, **so repent or turn-away from bad acts and know that Jesus has already died for that transgression and Father GOD has already forgotten it.**

Ephesians 5:1-2 Therefore be imitators of God, as beloved children. And walk in love, as Christ loved us and gave himself up for us, a fragrant offering and sacrifice to God.

- **<u>A New inheritance</u>.** This inheritance must be known and acted on to be manifested for the Believer. Listen as the Apostle Paul explains.

Sons and Heirs

Galatians 4:4-7 But when the **fullness of time** <u>had come</u> (<u>past tense</u>), God sent forth his Son, <u>born of woman</u>, <u>born under the law</u>, <u>to redeem those who were under the law</u>, <u>so that Believers might receive adoption as sons</u>. **And because <u>you are sons</u>, God has sent <u>the Spirit of his Son</u> into our hearts**, crying, "Abba! Father!" So you are no longer a slave, <u>but a son, and if a son</u>, **then an heir through God**.

Romans 8:16-17 The Spirit Himself bears witness with <u>our spirit</u> that we are the children of God. And if we are children, then **we are heirs**; **heirs of God** and **joint-heirs with Christ**; so that if we suffer <u>with *Him*</u>, we may also be glorified together.

<u>Context and fact of the New Inheritance for Believers</u>: The power to live **controlling the Believer's environment** <u>**requires knowledge of your inheritance**</u> **and <u>the renewing of your mind to the word of GOD</u>.** It is necessary to put into

action your inheritance. You are "Joint-heirs" with Jesus, meaning that Jesus must co-sign any time you want to use some of your inheritance. You must be of one mind to use your inheritance.

Every Believer is owner of all the inheritance from the Lord Jesus Christ but not all have reached a relationship with the Father GOD and Jesus to access the inheritance. Some Believers have not read the last Will and Testament of Jesus Christ and do not know what inheritance is theirs? Listen to the Apostle John give Believers a view of the starting of our eternal life as Christians.

1st John 5:13-15 I write these things to you **who believe** in the name of the Son of God that **you may know that you have eternal life**. And this is the confidence that we have toward him, that if we ask anything according to **his will,** he hears us. And if we know that he hears us in whatever we ask, **we know that we have the requests that we have asked of him.**

The New Testament is "the will" of Jesus Christ and you must know the terms of the Lord's will to receive its benefits.

Colossians 1:9-12 And so, from the day we heard, we have not ceased to pray for you, asking **that you may be filled with the knowledge of his will in all spiritual wisdom and understanding,** so as to walk in a manner worthy of the Lord, fully pleasing to him, bearing fruit in every good work and increasing in the knowledge of God. **May you be strengthened with all power,** according to his glorious might, for all endurance and patience with joy, giving thanks to the Father, **who has qualified you to share in the inheritance of the saints in light.**

The Apostle Paul's prayer for Believers is that we would be **filled with the knowledge of the Lord's will.**

3rd John 1:2 Beloved, in regard to all things I pray *that* you **prosper** and **be in health**, even **as your soul prospers**.

The <u>prospering of your soul</u> moves Believers into position to live inside the Lord's inheritance. The inheritance is, **control of your environment**, both Spiritual and physical; clothed in the Armor of GOD and consumed with the "Fruit of the Spirit". All the hidden inheritance of Christ is inside the Believer's Spirit and will be revealed by "GOD, the Holy Spirit" **for those that have ears to hear and eyes to see and a receptive heart**. <u>Think about this</u>, the hidden things, or the things to be revealed <u>are already inside you</u> waiting to be revealed or found.

- **<u>A New World</u> of the unseen**,

Not the physical world of the five senses but of GOD's eternal world for the Believer's newly created or re-born Spirit. <u>"The Eternal world of the Spirit" where GOD lives, where Believers can enjoy being a child of GOD in an environment controlled internally and externally by the Believer through the knowledge of GOD. Where Father God, Jesus Christ, and GOD, the Holy Spirit are "One with Believers"</u>. When you are one with the creator of the world, you are with the creator of the environment at its perfection.

Listen intently to Jesus speaking to GOD about Believers. When praying in the Garden of Gethsemane after the last supper.

John 17:14-26 And now I come to You, and these things I speak in the world **that (Believers) might have <u>My joy</u> fulfilled in them**. <u>I have given them Your Word</u>, and the world has hated them because <u>they are not of the world, even as I am not of the world.</u> I do not pray for You to take them out of the world, but <u>for You to keep them from the evil.</u>

Believers are **not** of the world, even as I am not of the world. Sanctify them through Your truth. **Your Word is truth**. As You have sent Me into the world, **even so I have sent them into the world**. And I sanctify Myself for their sakes, so that they also might be sanctified in truth. And I do not pray for these alone, **but for those also who shall believe on Me through their word**, that **they all** may be one, as You, Father, *are* in Me, and I in You, **that they also may be one in Us**, so that the world may believe that You have sent Me.

And **I have given them the glory** which You have given Me, that **they may be one, even as We are one, I in them, and You in Me**, that they may be made perfect in one; and that the world may know that You have sent Me and have loved them as You have loved Me. Father, I desire that *those* whom You have given Me, that they may be with Me where I am, that they may behold My glory which You have given Me, for You have loved Me before *the* foundation of *the* world. O righteous Father, indeed, the world has not known You; but I have known You, and these have known that You have sent me.

And I made known to them Your name, and will make *it* known, so that the love *with* which You have loved Me may be in them, and I in them.

Never let this prayer from Jesus out of your mind, think about the thoughts that Jesus, our Savior, had for Believers, Believers need to meditate on this prayer to understand all that it says. Think about this phrase, **"I have given Believers "the glory" which You have given Me, that they may be one, even as We are one, I in them, and You in Me, that they may be made perfect in One; and that the world may know that You have sent Me and have loved Believers as You have loved Me.** This statement is for **now**, not in Heaven".

Notice the "Oneness with GOD" expressed here <u>is to be done on earth.</u>

<u>Context</u> and fact. There is **a New World of the Spirit**. A Believer can go to the Throne of Grace and be in Jesus Christ and have Jesus inside the Believer in the realm of the physical world using their faith faculty, which GOD has given to every Believer, to live in the Spiritual world where GOD is while you are walking on earth.

- **<u>A "New Man or Woman"</u>** living in and through Christ.

<u>The New Life for the New Man.</u>

Ephesians 2:13-16 <u>But now in Christ Jesus</u> you who once were far off have been brought near by the blood of Christ. For he himself is our peace, who has <u>made us both one</u> and <u>has broken down in his flesh the dividing wall of hostility</u> by abolishing the law of commandments expressed in ordinances, **that he might create in himself <u>one new man</u>** <u>in place of the two,</u> so making peace and might reconcile us both to God in one body through the cross, thereby killing the hostility. (Jew and Gentile) (Believer and "GOD, the Holy Spirit")

<u>The old life.</u>

Ephesians 4:17-32 Now this I say and testify in the Lord, that <u>you must no longer walk as the Gentiles do,</u> **in the futility of their mind<u>s</u>**. They are darkened in their understanding, **alienated from <u>the life of God</u>** because of <u>the ignorance that is in them,</u> <u>due to their hardness of heart</u>. They have become callous and have <u>given themselves up</u> to sensuality, greedy, to practice every kind of impurity.

Put off the old life and be **renewed in the Spirit of your minds** and **put on the New Life**. Notice both scriptures speak of the mind of Christ and the Believer's mind, being one with GOD in our actions.

But that is not the way you learned Christ!—assuming that you have heard about him and were taught in him, as the truth is in Jesus, to put off your old self, which belongs to your former manner of life and is corrupt through deceitful desires, and **to be renewed** in **the spirit of your minds**, and to put on the new self, **created after the likeness of God in true righteousness and holiness.**

Give no opportunity to the Devil.

Therefore, having put away falsehood, let each one of you speak the truth with his neighbor, **for we are members one of another** (Body and Bride of Christ). Be angry and do not sin; do not let the sun go down on your anger, and give no opportunity to the devil. Let the thief no longer steal, but rather let him labor, doing honest work with his own hands, so that **he may have something to share with anyone in need.**

Words carry weight and should be controlled to only build up the hearer.

Let no corrupting talk come out of your mouths, but only such as is good for building up, as fits the occasion, **that it may give grace to those who hear**. And do not grieve the Holy Spirit of God, by whom you were sealed for the day of redemption. Let all bitterness and wrath and anger and clamor and slander be put away from you, along with all malice. Be kind to one another, tenderhearted, forgiving one another, as God in Christ forgave you.

Corrupting talk is anything that is not uplifting to you, the Believers hearing or to someone listening. **You can corrupt your own peace by speaking words that lead to chaos.**

- <u>**Jesus said, " My sheep hear my voice, I know them,**</u> **and they follow me."**

John 10:27-28 <u>My sheep hear my voice, and **I know them, and they follow me.**</u> I give them eternal life, and they will never perish, and no one will snatch them out of my hand.

Here are five ways GOD speaks to Believers: The first three are "General words from GOD" and the last two are "Specific words". <u>If you are **not** familiar with and using the "General words from GOD"</u> it is difficult to expect, GOD to give you a "Specific word" and Believers **to know how to hear and use it.**

1. Tuning your hearing to the voice of the Savior and **away from the enemy's weapons of fear, anxiety, and worry.**
2. Allowing your <u>GOD given conscience</u> to be your guide to right living and **not violating the direction of your conscience to do wrong or evil.**
3. Listening to the Word of GOD. The Bible is GOD's word speaking to you and **it is spirit** and **is life**. The word of GOD is full of the seeds of abundant life, **but the seeds must be planted in your heart** to grow into a fruit bearing tree.
4. Hearing from your Born-again Spirit through your mind<u>s</u> and checked before speaking or acting according to **the peace of GOD in your heart** for objective truth to act or speak.

5. Hearing and <u>expecting to hear</u> "GOD, the Holy Spirit" <u>speak through your being</u>, a voice, a thought, a scripture, a vision, a dream, or some other communique to indicate a proper path.

<u>**Context** and fact of Believers hearing the voice of the Lord.</u> **There is nothing standing between Believers and Father GOD and the Bible**, so what is keeping Believers from having a conversation with our brother, Savior, Lord, and GOD. Never forget, **the word of GOD "is GOD"** and that communication is waiting on you, to open it. Communication is a matter of <u>individual Believers tuning in and hearing the right channel.</u> **Too often Believers are tuning in and <u>hearing the enemy</u> with influences <u>to fear</u>, <u>to worry</u>, to <u>be afraid</u>, to <u>be anxious</u>, to constantly say <u>but, "what if"?</u>**

<u>Hearing from "GOD, the Holy Spirit" inside Believers is tuning your hearing to what GOD says to think about.</u>

- Tune your ears to hear what **the Spirit of GOD is saying**!
- <u>Rejoice in the Lord always</u>; again I will say, rejoice. Let your reasonableness (confidence) be known to everyone. *Philippians 4:4-8*
- <u>The Lord is at hand</u>; **do not be anxious about anything**, but in everything by prayer and supplication with thanksgiving let your requests be made known to God.
- **And the peace of God**, which surpasses all understanding, will guard your hearts and your minds in Christ Jesus.
- <u>Finally</u>, brothers, whatever <u>is true</u>, whatever is <u>honorable</u>, whatever is <u>just</u>, whatever is pure, whatever is <u>lovely</u>, whatever is <u>commendable</u>, if there is any

excellence, **<u>if there is anything worthy of praise, think about these things.</u>**

When Believers think about these thoughts, they will not think about worry, fear, or anxiety. The Apostle Paul is saying, constantly focus on your relationship with GOD, capturing and eliminating thoughts influenced by the enemy, and concentrating on the confidence you have in GOD. When Believers are thinking on these honorable things and living in "Oneness with GOD, whatever information you need for a GOD led plan is available.

Remember, the most basic communication from GOD is your conscience, inside every person there is a conscience of the knowledge of good and evil and right and wrong. Do not **violate your conscience** by choosing evil and wrong.

Conclusion. Each title in this section is taken from the quoted scripture that has been there for centuries. <u>How did we miss it for so long</u>? Do not miss the power of living your "eternal life" <u>now</u> with **a living Savior and GOD**. Believers who commit to this life will live the abundant life in Christ Jesus and will wake up every morning yearning for your new day with the Lord, through "GOD, the Holy Spirit" who raised Jesus from the dead and is inside you.

Listen to J B Phillips expound on Jesus being the object of our faith, not the outcome of our hope, connecting Believers with being "One with GOD" which is eternal life.

If My words <u>live in you</u>, THEN!

"Faith" to Jesus was <u>the fundamental fact</u>, a fact which once firmly grasped by heart and mind affects a man's life both here and in what we call "ETERNITY." Consider **His words**, "He that heareth my word, and believes on Him that sent me, *has* **everlasting life**" (Past tense. John 5:24). What is this faith but a plain assurance that if a man accepts the teaching of Christ as the fundamental expression of the Father's authority and plan, **he enters already upon that timeless quality of living which is called "eternal or everlasting life"**.

In other words, if a man uses his faith-faculty to grasp with heart and mind the essential truth about life, he becomes part of Real Life. The well-known words of Jesus, "**According to your faith be it unto you**" (Matthew 9:29), takes on a new meaning if we are thinking of faith, **not** as a desperate effort to believe, so much as the using of a faith faculty to grasp unseen realities and utilize unseen resources. There is a definite distinction between expressing a wish and **possessing a hope with real Bible grounds for it**. We must rid our minds of both **pious hopes and wishful thinking** before we get down to solid, genuine hope. That is, hope rooted **in the good "Purpose of God."**

Conclusion, "The Truth" and "The Gospel" could be described like this.

The GOSPEL of Jesus Christ is the fulfillment of GOD's plan for the coming of "The Messiah", the reversing of the penalty of sin, sickness, oppression, and separation from GOD and is the TRUTH. To Believers, Jesus returned the authority to reign on earth, Jesus restored GOD's glory to Believers, and gave the gift of "GOD, the Holy Spirit" to live inside Believers. And all this, so Believers could give GOD's love to their neighbor, and to the world, and be seen as the praise of GOD's glory.

It is so important; Believers must know and understand that **GOD loved and acted <u>first</u> to accept us into His Family.**

1st John 4:7-14 Beloved, let us love one another, <u>for love is from God</u>, and **whoever loves has been born of God and knows God**. Anyone who does not love does not know God, **<u>because God is love</u>**. <u>In this</u> the love of God was made manifest among us, **that God sent his only Son** into the world, so that <u>we might live through him</u>. <u>In this is love</u>, **<u>not</u> that we have loved God,** but that GOD loved us and sent his Son to be the propitiation for our sins. **<u>Beloved</u>, if God so loved us, we also ought to love one another.**

No one has ever seen God; **<u>if</u> we love one another, <u>God abides in us, and his love is perfected in us</u>**. By this we know that <u>we abide in him</u> and <u>he in us</u>, **because GOD has given us of his Spirit**. And we have seen and testify that the Father has sent his Son to be the Savior of the world.

Now let us take "Oneness with GOD" to the next level, let us consider "How do we worship GOD in Spirit and Truth?"

Chapter 4

Worship
Section 1. What is Worship?
Section 2. How do you worship in Spirit and Truth?

Worship is being "One with GOD", being motivated by loving GOD with all your heart, mind, soul, and strength and loving your neighbor in the same way GOD loves you. Underlying this edict, "the abundant life" is the result of living "One with GOD". Listen to the words of the Father and of Jesus.

Deuteronomy 11:1 "**You shall therefore "love" the LORD your God** and keep his charge, his statutes, his rules, and his commandments always.

Deuteronomy11:13 "And **if you will** indeed obey my commandments that I command you today, **"to love" the LORD your God, and to serve him with all your heart and with all your soul,**

Matthew 22:35-37 "Teacher, which is the great commandment in the Law?" And he said to him, "**You shall "love" the Lord your God with all your heart** and **with all your soul** and **with all your mind**.

Believers can only be "One with GOD" when Believers are focused on GOD, His word, and serving others. Listen to this word from Jesus.

John 15:3-7 Already you are clean **because of the word** that I have spoken to you. **Abide in me, and I in you.** As the branch cannot bear fruit by itself, unless it abides in the vine, **neither can you, unless you abide in me**. I am the vine; you are the branches. Whoever abides in me and I in him, he it is that bears much fruit, **for apart from me you can do nothing**. If anyone does not abide in me, he is thrown away like a branch and withers; and the branches are gathered, thrown into the fire, and burned. **If you abide in me, and my words abide in you, ask whatever you wish, and it will be done for you.**

Abiding with and acting on the words of Jesus is to hear from Jesus with your Spirit. "Abiding in Jesus" is the connection to worship or service and how we live our lives abiding in GOD's word because **GOD is His word and is Spirit**.

In this next verse, Jesus is telling the Pharisees that worship is **a thing of the heart** and **not** based on rituals and doctrines of men. So let us explore the words of Jesus to find doctrines of GOD that will enlighten us to worship, from our hearts and give Believers the knowledge of truth to keep us in every moment of our life.

Matthew 15:8-9 (Jesus describing the Jewish people,) This people draws nigh unto me **with their mouth**, and honors me with *their* lips; but **their heart is far from me**. But **in vain** they do worship me, teaching *for* **doctrines** the commandments of men. Now a word from Father GOD about your new heart.

Deuteronomy 30:6 And the LORD your **God will circumcise your heart** and the heart of your offspring, **so that** you will **love the LORD your God with all your heart and with all your soul**, that you may live.

Worship is a product of the heart; it starts from the inner parts of Believers and controls Believers thoughts and actions. Worship is serving and adoring GOD, **as a way of life**, a love affair with GOD. A committed reality that involves your life being "One with GOD", as a way of life. So how do we become "One with GOD"?

A premise for us to ponder, Father GOD asked Abraham to sacrifice his son, whom he loved, and Abraham called **the**

obedience to serve GOD and the action of sacrifice, "worship".

Let us examine the first time the word "worship" is used in the Bible to establish a starting point for the meaning of worship. Abraham had been asked by GOD to go to a place and sacrifice his only son, whom he loved.

Genesis 22:3-5 In the morning Abraham got up and saddled his donkey. He took Isaac and two servants with him. He cut the wood for the sacrifice. Then they went to the place where God told them to go. After they traveled three days, Abraham looked up, and in the distance, he saw the place where they were going. Then he said to his servants, "Stay here with the donkey. The boy and I will go to that place and **worship**. Then **"we" will come** back to you later."

Worship or service seems costly, but it is not, it is the "true alignment of a Believers heart and mind" to a relationship with Father GOD "with all of who you are" and "who GOD is to you". The Apostle Paul tells us later that Abraham had faith in GOD to resurrect his son, to keep GOD's promise. Do we believe GOD or do we believe in a GOD? Abraham believed GOD and His word. Now think about worship, **as the service, we see Jesus' exhibit to the world**.

The Apostle Paul said, "I call on you through the compassions of God to present your bodies a living sacrifice, holy, pleasing to God, *which is* **your reasonable service**".

These examples from Jesus and Abraham are the heart of worship. Both examples ask for the very heart of our being and priority of the Believers actions to be a way of life. Scripture makes clear that after the resurrection, GOD desired to know all Believers and be part of our lives through sending "GOD, the Holy Spirit" to lead, guide, and tell us of things to come. The Greek word for Holy Spirit as a comforter is "para cletos" which means joined at the hip or to come along side. Currently not many Believer's testimonies reflect a partnership with "GOD, the Holy Spirit" in their lives.

Worship is love and love,
Must be expressed with action and communication.

TO be "One with GOD" the motivation for our entire life must be about our <u>relationship with GOD</u>, <u>for others</u>, and <u>not for ourselves</u>. This makes very little sense to us, who are in this physical world trying to live in a world bombarding Believers to live a selfish life. <u>So, we must go further in our study</u>, to find out how to be **in** this world **but <u>not be of this world</u>**. Think about this statement, Jesus has sent Believers into the world as Jesus was sent into the world, "One with GOD" and "GOD, the Holy Spirit" remained on him.

The preacher at church cannot be a Believers substitute for hearing from GOD in the Believers daily life. Israel told Moses they did not want to talk to GOD anymore, after their first experience, and they wanted Moses to talk to GOD and relay GOD's words back to them. Cutting yourself off from a personal relationship with GOD and having someone go to GOD for you is a failed exercise and is not GOD's plan. Jesus said, "My sheep hear my voice, I know them, and they follow me." *John 10:27* <u>Every Believer must answer this question</u>, is Jesus your shepherd, and if so, "What is He saying to you?"

The word "Christ", is one of the descriptive names of the Lord Jesus, signifying the "Anointed of JEHOVAH" and this Hebrew word is the same word as "Messiah". In the original Hebrew, the name "Christ", specifically and particularly, means the union of <u>both natures</u> in the person, <u>both divine and human</u>; and as such becoming a "Christ-ian" is to be, **"One with GOD"**. It is becoming "One mind with GOD" that is uniting our will with the will of GOD, the priority of the Christian lifestyle.

Believers must take a new look at "Worship" and being "One with GOD" to understand the Apostle Paul **when he says**, **"<u>pray unceasingly</u>"**, or **"<u>in all things give thanks</u>"**, or "<u>let us **continually offer up a sacrifice of praise to God**, that is, the fruit of lips</u>" or "**<u>give your bodies as a living sacrifice</u>** is your <u>reasonable service</u>". All these instructions for living require a 24/7 commitment, which is impossible to do without it being part of the Believers lifestyle.

The ability to do these actions can be stifled by the Believers refusal to embrace the gift of "GOD, the Holy Spirit". Believers cannot be likeminded with GOD and **<u>not</u>** have a relationship with "GOD, the Holy Spirit" inside your being. Refusing to relate to GOD's gift of His Spirit is a selfish act of rebellion, fear of the unseen, or lack of knowledge of GOD's word, **leaving Believers to live their life, in their own power yielding man-made results.**

Where is the Treasure that motivates your life?

Jesus warns Believers that <u>where we find our treasure</u>, we will also find our heart. Believers wanting to be "One with GOD" need for GOD to be our treasure. Listen closely to the parable, " the pearl of great price" from two perspectives:

The Parable of, " The Pearl of Great Value".

Matthew 13:45-46 **Jesus speaking**, Again, the Kingdom of Heaven is like unto a merchant man, seeking goodly pearls: **Who, when he had found one pearl of great price**, went, and <u>sold all that he had, and bought it.</u>

<u>Perspectives.</u>

    1. Would you sell all of yourself, to find the GOD of the Universe?

    2. Jesus found in Mankind "the pearl of great price" and <u>gave His all to buy you and me.</u>

It is hard to look in the mirror and see our humanity and then comprehend the love GOD has for Believers, **but we are missing the point**: GOD, <u>is a parent</u>, and loves **"whose we are"** not "<u>what we are</u>". <u>When we choose Jesus, as Savior, our Spirits are made in the **exact image of GOD,** and we are the beautiful **offspring of GOD**</u>. (Not in our bodies or souls, but in our Spirit.)

Let us examine another descriptive term about relating to GOD, "adore". GOD adores His Children, what can we learn from this adoration? Let us look at the definition of "Adore" when speaking about GOD and see if this will help us evaluate the motivation of our worship and service lifestyle.

By the act of <u>adoration of GOD</u> is implied the full and most absolute **acknowledgment of worth** <u>and by right</u> can only be suitable or proper to offer exclusively to Almighty God **<u>who made everything.</u>**

Believers who adore GOD are also doers: listen to the following two translations of Ephesians 5:1-2 and notice <u>the consuming life</u> of "walking in love" as <u>Jesus has loved us</u>.

Ephesians 5:1-2 Therefore be followers of God, <u>as dear children</u>. And **walk in love**, as <u>Christ also has loved us</u>, and has given Himself for us as an offering and a sacrifice to God for a sweet-smelling savor. MKJV

Ephesians 5:1-2 Therefore **be imitators of God**, as <u>beloved children</u>. And <u>walk in love</u>, as Christ loved us and gave himself up for us, <u>a fragrant offering and sacrifice to God</u>. ESV

Did you see, Jesus is saying, **beloved children** be committed to GOD as a sweet smelling offering to Father GOD. To imitate or be a follower of Jesus is to be devoted to GOD with our lives allowing the leadership of "GOD, the Holy Spirit" and GOD's word to be our motivation 24/7 at work, at home, and at play. Believers loving life as we serve others and have our "being" in Christ. **Now that is worship** or said in another way **love expressed in action**.

Listen to the writer of Hebrews as he separates the inward devotion to GOD with the "also phrase" do good and share with others for such is pleasing to GOD.

Hebrews 13:15 Through Jesus then let us **<u>continually</u> offer up <u>a sacrifice of praise to God</u>**, that is, the fruit of our lips that acknowledge his name. **Do not neglect to do good and to share** what you have, for such sacrifices are pleasing to God.

As Believers, all the actions, offerings, or sacrifices we do for our church and community, being led by the Spirit with a motivation of love for your neighbor **are perfect and are the hallmark of a worship lifestyle**.

Now let us think about the Apostle Peter's words to the lame man at the Gate Beautiful.

Acts 3:6-7 Silver and gold have I none; **but such as I have give I to you**: In the name of Jesus Christ of Nazareth **rise up and walk**. And he took him by the right hand and lifted *him* up: and immediately his feet and ankle bones received strength.

How does "such as I have, I give to you" work in your life? Do you ever say, "in the name of Jesus" standing in your mandate to go into the world as Jesus was sent into the world. I did not write this to shame anyone but to inspire Believers and myself to the life Jesus wants Believers to live. Believers are the Lord's representative in the earth, and we can stand and proclaim the word of GOD in the Name of Jesus Christ and know we are authorized to speak in His Name, minister healing in His name, minister deliverance in His name, and more.

Can you feel the building of verse upon verse creating the picture of dedicating every thought and action to GOD because it is the greater way to live and GOD is "Adorable": adoring and being devoted to GOD is the only way to, "Be in this world, but **not** be of this world". If you think this is uncomfortable, brace yourself.

Worship is more than the connection with GOD during the music service before the sermon on Sunday. Ask yourself, "how do you worship a Spirit?" and "how do you worship GOD in Spirit and Truth?" Think about it, "Truth" is not a Sunday only concept, but is 24/7. The short answer to "How to worship in Spirit and Truth is **to live in the Spirit realm of life with GOD, all the time.** The word, "Worship" in the Greek language is the combination of the word "worth" and "vessel" or worth-ship.

"GET on BOARD with GOD." Your relationship with GOD must be the priority to your life, your direction, and your actions. The Apostle Paul uses the word, "Beholding GOD", a beautiful future perfect tense action that is on-going. How do you see GOD, what is GOD to you? Do you realize GOD is interested in you all week. Are Believers, thrown off course, by the fact, that GOD's Holy Spirit is inside Believers? **Do you** as a Believer know about and believe in "GOD, the Holy Spirit"?

Now let us look at the way the words "spirit and truth" appear in the Bible. Truth was coupled with other words, other than Spirit, in the Old Testament. Notice in the Old Testament the most used coupler is "mercy and Truth" because "Grace and Truth" came through Jesus Christ. Notice, there is <u>not</u> one reference to a negative term coupled with truth.

The Old Testament words coupled with "Truth".

Exodus 34:6 .... Jehovah God, merciful and gracious, long-suffering, and abundant in <u>goodness and truth,</u>

Joshua 24:14 Now, then, <u>fear Jehovah, and serve Him</u> in <u>sincerity and truth.</u>

2nd Samuel 2:6 And now may Jehovah <u>do kindness and truth</u> <u>to you.</u>

2nd Samuel …. May <u>mercy and truth</u> be with you.

2nd Kings 20:19 … <u>Good *is* the Word of Jehovah which you</u> <u>have spoken.</u> And he said, *is it* not *good* if <u>peace and truth</u> are in my days?

Esther 9:30 And he sent the letters to all the Jews, to the hundred and twenty-seven provinces of the kingdom of Ahasuerus, <u>*with* words of peace and truth.</u>

Psalms 25:10 All the paths of Jehovah *are* <u>mercy and truth to</u> <u>those who keep His covenant and His testimonies.</u>

Psalms 61:7 He shall abide before God forever; prepare <u>mercy and truth</u> to preserve him.

Psalms 85:10 <u>Mercy and truth have met together;</u> <u>righteousness and peace have kissed *each other*.</u>

Psalms 86:15 But You, O God, *are* <u>God full of pity, and</u> <u>gracious, long-suffering, and rich in mercy and truth.</u>

Psalms 89:14 Justice and judgment *are* the foundation of <u>Your throne;</u> <u>mercy and truth</u> shall go before Your face.

Proverbs 3:3-4 Let not <u>mercy and truth</u> forsake you; <u>tie them</u> <u>around your neck; write them upon the tablet of your heart;</u> and <u>you shall find favor and good understanding in the sight</u> <u>of God and man.</u>

Proverbs 14:22 Do not those who think evil go astray? But mercy and truth shall be to those who think of good.

Proverbs 16:6 By mercy and truth, iniquity is purged, and by the fear of Jehovah *men* turn away from evil.

Proverbs 20:28 Mercy and truth preserve the king; and his throne is upheld by mercy.

Isaiah 39:8 … Good *is* the Word of Jehovah which you have spoken. And he said, for there shall be peace and truth in my days.

Jeremiah 33:6 Behold, I will bring it health and healing, and I will heal them and will show them the riches of peace and truth.

Each couplet is attached to a favorable outcome, Notice the last one, "I will heal them and show them the riches of "peace and truth".

**In the New Testament.
"Spirit and Truth" is first mentioned in John 4,**

New Testament words coupled with "truth."

John 1:17 For the law was given through Moses; **grace and truth** came through Jesus Christ.

John 4:23 But the hour is coming, and now is, when the true worshipers shall worship the Father **in spirit and truth**, for the Father seeks such to worship Him.

John 4:24 God *is* a spirit, and they who worship Him must worship in **spirit and in truth.**

1st Corinthians 5:8 Therefore let us keep *the* feast; not with old leaven, nor with the leaven of malice and wickedness, but with the unleavened *bread* of **sincerity and truth**.

Ephesians 5:9 (for the fruit of the Spirit *is* in all goodness and **righteousness and truth),**

1st Timothy 2:3-7 For this *is* good and acceptable in the sight of God our Savior, who will have all men to be saved and to come to the knowledge of the truth. For God *is* one, and *there is* one Mediator of God and of men, *the* Man Christ Jesus, who gave Himself a ransom for all, to be testified in due time, to this I am ordained a preacher and an apostle (I speak the truth in Christ, I do not lie), a teacher of *the* nations, in **faith and truth**.

It is evident that "truth" is GOD's plan for the moment, the day, and forever and is our steadfast anchor. The reason we must worship GOD in the Spirit is because **our Spirit is the only part of Believers worthy to approach GOD**. The reason we worship in Truth is Jesus, **who is the Messiah sent by GOD, is Truth** and Jesus is the only way to the Father and **is now Spirit**.

How do Believers increase our momentum to change, Knowing that GOD does not need to change?

Now, listen to the Apostle Paul as he begs Believers to be a "Living Sacrifice", which is the Believer's worship (or service) in Spirit and Truth and this devotion is achieved by the renewal of your mind revealing the good, acceptable, and perfect will of GOD for your actions. Think about this, Your Spirit is perfect and includes the mind of Christ, and "GOD, the Holy Spirit" is inside Believers, but our natural mind and brain **restrict** the perfect will of GOD from being accomplished by a lack of knowledge of GOD, His word, and the Believers confidence in our authority as Ambassadors to the Kingdom of GOD's dear Son. Listen to the convicting worlds of the Apostle Paul.

Romans 12:1-2 I appeal to you therefore, brothers, by the mercies of God, to present your bodies as a living sacrifice, holy (set apart from the world systems) and acceptable to God, which is your spiritual worship. Do not be conformed to this world, but **be transformed by the renewal of your mind**, that by testing (your thoughts) you may discern what is the will of God, what is good and acceptable and perfect. ESV

John 4:24 **God is Spirit**, and those who worship him **must worship in Spirit and Truth."**

If you find a word for a situation in your life, **in the Bible**, it is a **word from GOD** and **it is Spirit**. When Believers do not have a connection with their born-again Spirit and "GOD, the Holy Spirit", they must rely on the Bible and the peace of GOD in their heart to guide their lives.

Now listen to the Apostle Paul as he dedicates Christians to Jesus, like a bride is given to her husband, but watch and be aware of deceiving people and thoughts that lead you away from "Oneness with GOD".

2nd Corinthians 11:2-3 For I feel a divine jealousy for you, since I betrothed you to one husband, to present you as a pure virgin to Christ. But I am afraid that as the serpent deceived Eve by his cunning, **your thoughts will be led astray from a sincere and pure devotion to Christ**.

It is evident from scripture, devotion and adoration to GOD is the platform Believers must use to follow Jesus and be aware of the enemies lies to lead Believers astray. **Now**, can scripture help us unlock the intent of the words, **"we must worship GOD in spirit and truth"**? Listen to the words of Jesus to the woman at the well, Jesus reveals there <u>is no longer **a place** to worship</u>, the only requirement is that worship be from our hearts and in "Spirit and Truth".

John 4:20-25 <u>The woman at the well speaking</u>, our fathers worshiped on this mountain, but you say that in Jerusalem is the place where people ought to worship." Jesus said to her, "Woman, believe me, the hour is coming when **neither** <u>on this mountain nor in Jerusalem</u> <u>will you worship the Father. You worship what you do not know</u>; we worship what we know, for salvation is from the Jews.

<u>But the hour is coming</u>, <u>and **is now here**</u>, when <u>the true worshipers</u> **will worship the Father in spirit and truth**, for the Father is seeking such people to worship him. **<u>God is spirit, and those who worship him must worship in spirit, and in truth</u>**.

<u>GOD's design of the world systems</u> works according to the principles of **"being One with GOD"** and serving others with love. The reason the Believers Spirit is filled with love, joy, peace, patience, goodness, faithfulness, temperance, and self-control are the qualities of the Spirit life and are the pictures of GOD in Believers. **GOD installed "The Fruit of the Spirit" in the Believer, so that Believers can control your environment both in your inner self and your physical surroundings with the power of the GOD's word and GOD's Spirit.**

Chapter 5

**Belief determines <u>where</u> you spend eternity.
and Behavior determines <u>how</u> you spend your eternity.**

This chapter is an in-depth look at the words <u>completed</u>, <u>finished</u>, and <u>perfected</u> used to describe the works of our Savior. Each word in this study is translated from the same Greek word. These words are all associated with the works of Jesus and the works are all **past tense**. At some point, everyone needs to come to the realization that they need a savior and <u>a change from living for themselves</u> **to living for and with the GOD of the Universe.** Listen to hear what the Apostle Paul writes about where mankind was before and after Jesus.

Romans 5:1-6 Therefore, since we have been justified by faith, we have peace with God through our Lord Jesus Christ. Through Jesus we have also obtained access by faith (Undeserved privilege) into this grace in which we stand, <u>and we rejoice in hope of the glory of God</u>. Not only that, but we rejoice in our sufferings,<u> knowing that suffering produces endurance, and endurance produces character, and character produces hope, and hope does not put us to shame,</u> **because God's love has been poured into our hearts through <u>the Holy Spirit who has been given to us.</u>**

For while we were still sinners, at the right time <u>Christ died for the ungodly</u>.

1st Corinthians 1:30-31 And because of him you are in Christ Jesus, <u>who became to Believers</u> **wisdom from God**, **righteousness** and **sanctification** and **redemption**, so that, as it is written, "Let the one who boasts, boast in the Lord."

Now listen as the Apostle Paul chastises the Ephesians who have added to the Gospel of Jesus Christ.

Ephesians 4:20-25 But that is not the way you learned Christ!—assuming that you have heard about Jesus and were taught in him, as <u>the truth is in Jesus</u>, to **put off your old self**, which <u>belongs to your former manner of life</u> and <u>is corrupt through deceitful desires</u>, and to **be renewed in the spirit of your minds**, and to **put on the new self**, <u>created after the likeness of God in true righteousness and holiness</u>. Therefore, having put away falsehood, let each one of you speak the truth with his neighbor, for <u>we are members one of another.</u>

You are the righteousness of Jesus Christ, rejoice and enjoy, and live right by receiving GOD's love and presence in every life situation. GOD is inside you watching Your words and actions whether you want Him to watch or not.

Believers are perfected by belief in "who Jesus is".
and "who Believers are" because of "who Jesus is".

<u>Believers cannot be perfected by behavior</u>, but **we are perfected** <u>when we behave according to the love in our hearts from GOD</u>. The following section is a word study of the Greek word "Telios, and Teleo" translated <u>perfected, completed,</u> and <u>finished</u>. These three translated aspects of the Greek word are used to describe the finished, completed, and perfected works of the Lord with His death, burial, and resurrection. These words speak to the grandeur of the works of Jesus and to <u>the Believers inclusion into the family of GOD.</u>

Luke 13:32 And Jesus said unto them, Go and say to that fox (Herod), **Behold**, <u>I cast out demons and perform cures</u> **to-day** and **to-morrow**, and **the third *day* I am perfected.**

John 17:23 (Jesus speaking) I in them and you in me, <u>that they may become</u> **perfectly one**, so that <u>the world may know that you sent me and</u> **loved them even as you loved me**.

Matthew 5:48 You therefore **shall be perfect**, as your heavenly Father <u>is</u> **perfect**. (Future)

Hebrews 2:10-11 But we see Jesus, who *was* made a little lower than the angels for the suffering of death, crowned with glory and honor, **that He by** *the* **grace of God** should taste death for all. For it became Him, for whom *are* all things and by whom *are* all things, in bringing many sons into glory, **to perfect the Captain of their salvation** <u>through sufferings</u>.

Hebrews 5:7-8 And **being made perfect**, <u>he (Jesus) became the source of eternal salvation to all who obey him, being designated by God a high priest</u> after the order of Melchizedek.

Hebrews 7:27-28 since he did <u>this once for all</u> when he offered up himself. For the law appoints men in their weakness as high priests, but the word of the oath, which came later than the law, **appoints a Son** <u>**who has been made perfect forever**</u>.

Hebrews 10:1 For since the law has but a shadow of the good things to come instead of the true form of these realities, <u>it can never</u>, by the same sacrifices that are continually offered every year, **make perfect those who draw near**. Otherwise, would they not have ceased to be offered, <u>since the worshipers, having once been cleansed, would no longer have any consciousness of sins?</u>

Hebrews 10:12-14 But <u>when Christ had offered for all time a single sacrifice for sins</u>, **he sat down at the right hand of God,** waiting from that time until his enemies should be made a footstool for his feet. <u>For by a single offering, he has **perfected for all time** those who are being sanctified.</u>

Hebrews 12:23 and to the assembly of the firstborn who are enrolled in heaven, and to God, the judge of all, and <u>to the spirits of the righteous **made perfect**, and to Jesus, the mediator of a new covenant, and to the sprinkled blood that speaks a better word than the blood of Abel.</u>

Psalms 18:30 *As for* God, **his way** *is* **perfect**: the word of the LORD is tried: he *is* a buckler to all those that trust in him.

Psalms 19:7 **The law of the LORD** *is* **perfect**, converting the soul: the testimony of the LORD *is* sure, making wise the simple.

"Finished" same Greek root word as "perfected".

John 19:30 When Jesus had received the sour wine, he said, **"It is finished,"** and he bowed his head and **gave up his spirit**.

John 17:4 I have glorified You (Father) upon the earth. **I have finished** the work which You have given Me to do.

"Completed" in Him same Greek word as "perfected".

Colossians 2:9-14 For in Him dwells all the fullness of the Godhead bodily. <u>And **you are complete in Him**</u>, who is the Head of all principality and power, in whom also you are circumcised with the circumcision made without hands, in putting off the <u>body of the sins of the flesh</u> by the circumcision of Christ, buried with Him in baptism, in whom also you were raised <u>through the faith of the working of God, raising Him (Jesus) from the dead</u>. And you, being dead in your sins and the uncircumcision of your flesh, **He has made alive together with Him, having forgiven you all trespasses, blotting out the handwriting of ordinances that was against us, which was contrary to us, and has taken it out of the way, nailing it to the cross.**

Believers are <u>not</u> perfected <u>with our performance</u>, but we are **perfected, completed, or finished** <u>in our position with GOD.</u> When Believers are living in a relationship with GOD, prioritizing GOD's will over our will and not living through the appetites of our flesh we can enjoy the Divine Nature of GOD. And all this is a gift from a loving GOD.

2nd Peter 1:2-4 Grace and peace be multiplied to you <u>through the knowledge of God</u> and of Jesus our Lord, according **as His divine power** has **given to us all things that *pertain* to life and godliness**, <u>through the knowledge of Him</u> who has called us to glory and virtue, through which <u>He has given to us exceedingly great and precious promises</u>, **so that by these you might be partakers of *the* divine nature**, having escaped the corruption *that is* in *the* world through lust.

Conclusion with another view from the Apostle Paul.

Romans 13:12 The night is far gone; the day is at hand. So then let us cast off the works of darkness and **put on the armor of light**. Let us walk properly, as in the daytime, <u>not in orgies and drunkenness, not in sexual immorality and sensuality, not in quarreling and jealousy. **But put on the Lord Jesus Christ**</u>, and <u>make no provision for the flesh</u>, to gratify its desires.

How strong is that. Put on the Lord Jesus and **make <u>no</u> provision** <u>for the flesh, to gratify its desires</u>.

Section 2

Put off your old self and put on your new self.

And now a section of Scripture adding to the word study of the Lord's finished, completed, and perfected promises for all Believers, Born-again of His Spirit, and given the authority and power to follow Jesus.

**Believers are children of GOD.
What do you think of your Heavenly Father?**

When Believers are born again, we become "New creatures" in our Spirits. Our Spirit is made in image of GOD and is identical to Jesus. Listen to the Apostle Paul

2ⁿᵈ Corinthians 5:17 Therefore, if anyone is in Christ, he is a new creation. The old (man) has passed away; **behold, the new (Spirit) has come.**

1ˢᵗ Corinthians 6:17 But he who is joined to the Lord **becomes one Spirit with Him.**

1ˢᵗ John 4:17. By this is love perfected with us, so that we may have confidence for the day of judgment, because **as "Jesus is"** so also are **we** in this world.

The warning that goes with this truth is, do not allow your physical mind and your mind of Christ in your Spirit to be double minded **for you can do nothing without Christ**, therefore examine your motivation for any action, to be of the same mind as Jesus. James 1:8 and 4:8.

The Believer's new Spirit is created in righteousness and true holiness.

Ephesians 4:22-24. as <u>the truth is in Jesus, to put off your old self, which belongs to your former manner of life</u> and is corrupt through deceitful desires, and **to be renewed in the spirit of your mind<u>s</u>**, and <u>to put on the new self, created after the likeness of God in true righteousness and holiness.</u>

Are you stacking scripture on scripture to see the depth of what our Heavenly Father wants Believers to experience with GOD every day, not only on Sunday, but every day.

Our New Spirit is sealed with "GOD, the Holy Spirit" and sin cannot penetrate the seal. Our Spirits are perfect and cannot sin. Our Spirits are the only part of Believers qualified to communicate with GOD.

Ephesians 1:13-14 In him you also, when you heard the word of truth, <u>the gospel of your salvation,</u> and believed in him, **were sealed** with the **promised Holy Spirit**, who is the guarantee of our inheritance until we acquire possession of it, to the praise of GOD's glory.

1ˢᵗ John 3:9 <u>Everyone who has been born of God</u> **does not commit sin**, because GOD's (immutable) seed remains in him, and **he cannot sin**, <u>because he has been born of God.</u>

1ˢᵗ John 4:4 You are of God, little children, and have overcome them (those with the spirit of anti-christ) : **because greater is he that is in you, than he that is in the world.**

Do you know "who" and "what" you are?
GOD only sees two TYPES of people:
Believers and unbelievers.

Believers are now the "Temple of GOD", and the "Kingdom of GOD" is inside the Believer's Spirit. **GOD is love, GOD is His word, and the Word is GOD, and we are His Children.**

Scripture speaks of GOD having hands, a face and eyes and ears, and Jesus became flesh, but God, the Father, is a Spirit. So, when GOD says, "Let us make man in our image and likeness", GOD is referring to Believers being Spirit beings. (*Exodus 7:5, 33:22-23, 33:20 and 23, 2nd Chronicles 7:15, John 1:14*)

Obviously, we have physical bodies to accommodate living in this atmosphere, but **we are Spirit beings made in GOD's image** living inside a body. The ages past, saw GOD manifest Himself more in the physical realm and during the age of our Savior, GOD was with Believers in Jesus, the person, but now in the age of the Church, GOD is with every Believer sealed as part of the Family of GOD by "GOD, the Holy Spirit".

Think about it, we are now living **Spirit to Spirit with GOD**, if we believe GOD and look to be likeminded, we will know His Presence. GOD is present inside us for every deed and every thought and every word we say. How scarry is that! But GOD would not offer Believers "GOD, the Holy Spirit" if this "Oneness with GOD" was not GOD's plan **and for our benefit.**

My immediate thought "is" living in the lifestyle described as worship and service would have eliminated most every problem I have ever encountered, and if I start now, my life and the lives around me will be better. Listen to the way King David wrote about **the one thing** that is important. **Seek after His face, dwell in His house, and gaze upon the beauty of the**

Lord; that is David's lifestyle and should be every Believers lifestyle.

The Lord Is My Light and My Salvation.
A Psalm from David

Psalms 27 The LORD is my light and my salvation; **whom shall I fear**? The LORD is the **stronghold of my life**; of whom shall I be afraid? When evildoers assail me to eat up my flesh, my adversaries, and foes, it is they who stumble and fall. Though an army encamp against me, my heart shall not fear; though war arise against me, **yet I will be confident**. **"One thing" have I asked of the LORD**, that will I seek after: **that I may dwell in the house of the LORD all the days of my life, to gaze upon the beauty of the LORD and to inquire in his temple.**

For he will hide me in his shelter in the day of trouble; he will conceal me under the cover of his tent; he will lift me high upon a rock. And now my head shall be lifted up above my enemies all around me, and I will offer in his tent sacrifices with shouts of joy; **I will sing and make melody to the LORD**. Hear, O LORD, when I cry aloud; be gracious to me and answer me! You have said, **"Seek my face." My heart says to you, "Your face, LORD, do I seek." Hide not your face from me.**

Turn not your servant away in anger, O you who have been my help. Cast me not off; forsake me not, **O God of my salvation**! For my father and my mother have forsaken me, but the LORD will take me in. Teach me your way, O LORD, and lead me on a level path because of my enemies. Give me not up to the will of my adversaries; for false witnesses have risen against me, and they breathe out violence. **I believe** that I shall look upon the goodness of the LORD in the land of the living! Wait for the LORD; be strong and let your heart take courage; wait for the LORD!

When I read the Psalms David wrote, I know my relationship needs to grow and become the priority of every moment of my life. **Meditate along with me, toward becoming "One with GOD" uniting the mind of our flesh with the mind of Christ in our Spirit and being completely confident that it is not I that lives but Christ lives in me.**

GOD has lifted Believers up to His level in the Spirit realm. Certainly, GOD, the Father, has and is doing mighty miracles through Believers daily on the earth. **But GOD's desire for Believers is to relate to Him through the Spirit instead of our senses and live in Divine health, peace, prosperity, and contentment.** Can you imagine having the relationship with GOD described in the next three verses?

1st Corinthians 6:19-20 You should know that your body is a temple for the Holy Spirit that you received from God and that (GOD) lives in you. You don't own yourselves. God paid a very high price to make you his. So, honor God with your body.

Ephesians 3:14-19 For this reason I bow my knees before the Father, from whom every family in heaven **and on earth is named**, that according to the riches of GOD's glory He may grant you to be strengthened with power through his Spirit **in your inner being**, so **that Christ may dwell in your hearts** through faith—that you, being rooted and grounded in love, may have strength to comprehend with all the saints what is the breadth and length and height and depth, and **to know the love of Christ** that surpasses knowledge, that you may be filled with all the fullness of God.

Ephesians 3:20-21 **Now to him** who is able to do far more abundantly than all that we ask or think, **according to the**

<u>**power at work within us,**</u> <u>to him be glory in the church and in Christ Jesus</u> throughout all generations, forever and ever.

Notice, this is so powerful in shaping our thoughts, **"we are the offspring of GOD, because of Jesus Christ."** And **there is power inside Believers** revealed by "GOD, the Holy Spirit".

The "New Hour is Here" Believers have a new Spirit made in the image of GOD and GOD is asking us to communicate with The Father of all Creation from our Spirit. Believers are now Citizens of Heaven and GOD wants to interact with His children. It doesn't matter what is said or what question we ask, or what praise we offer, or what song we sing, or our physical attitude: it seems only to matter that our speech, thoughts, and actions is from our heart or Spirit and is for our Father and His other children. **Adoring our Father with our words, thoughts, and actions is worship and is service**. Communicating from our Spirit to GOD, will align our actions with GOD's will and let Christ live in Believers, likeminded with the mind of Christ.

Let me describe the opposite of **"it is <u>not</u> I living but Christ living in me"**. Have you ever gone to work worried about money, relationships, or failures of every kind? Worry and anxiety <u>are the Devils communication</u> with you. When the communications of worry and anxiety happen to Christians, you are tuned into the wrong station and by definition, **are <u>not</u> talking to GOD,** who offers the abundant life and peace. **The enemy of our peace and rest in the Lord** <u>are the lies from the Devil</u> **that our GOD is not enough. Our GOD is more than enough and is speaking to His children all day every day and GOD cares**. Find GOD's channel, sing his songs, listen to his words, think about His promises, and talk to Him.

I want to see Jesus followers find the passion for GOD that I see on Sunday at the NFL games, how about you? A picture of <u>worldly</u> worship can be seen on television on Sundays at the professional football games. People sleeping out at a stadium, with painted faces and crazy outfits and tailgating parties of extraordinary expense, fans dedicating their time, allegiance, and money to the team of their choice with absolutely no lasting return. This worship is idolatry.

At churches where GOD's power is evident, tailgating may become popular. The Lord is pouring out His Spirit on all flesh, let the Spirit filled life become fashionable.

Chapter 6

GOD's communication with Believers
is from inside Believers, not outside.

Questions. Why do many prayers go unanswered? If "GOD, the Holy Spirit" is inside Believers, can't we just talk with GOD? Is the answer to all prayer in the Bible? If GOD knows what we have need of before we pray, why pray?

How does GOD communicate with Believers? The word says GOD has written his instruction on Believers new heart or Spirit. The Apostle Paul says that the Believer's life and the Lord's inheritance of the Saints is <u>hidden in the Spirit of Believers</u>. So, the communication with Believers from GOD must be from inside you. Here are four ways to hear GOD and follow Him.

You have heard the saying, "**let your conscience be your guide**", your conscience is the voice of the knowledge of Good and evil. It is the first way to hear what GOD would suggest that you do, without compromising your free-will to do what you choose to do. **Your conscience knows right from wrong**. If you truly follow the path the Lord illuminates, you have done well and will be blessed. If you choose the direction not illuminated by the Lord, you will wander into the darkness and will be acting in man-made power.

The Bible has hundreds of specific instructions directly from Jesus and many from the Apostle Paul written for instruction, correction, rebuke, and teaching. There is a list of 50 or so communiques from Jesus and Paul in the section following on prayer. Everything the Lord communicates to His children is cloaked in His love for the world and will lead you into green pastures by the still water.

If you are seeking confirmation of a plan or idea from your mind? Consider this, when your mind is "one" with the mind of Christ in your Spirit, your mind will grasp Spiritual communications from GOD and confirm your direction. Also, the written word stored in your heart is the voice of GOD and the Believer can have confidence in the written word to act. All thoughts need to be measured against the love of GOD and let the peace of GOD rule in your heart when evaluating a word or an action. *Colossians 3:14-15*

"GOD, the Holy Spirit" when questioned or invited, will speak, communicate, lead, or stop a failed path if Believers communicate. **Jesus guaranteed that His sheep hear His voice, know Him, and follow Him.**

In the time, after Jesus had ascended to sit next to Father GOD to advocate for Believers, the aspects of prayer changed. Jesus finished, completed, and perfected the new way to live as a child of GOD, all the promises Jesus made are perfected and available for Believer's use and the new look to prayer is to have faith in the promises Jesus had faith to complete. For example, Believers can appropriate the benefits of Salvation: healing, deliverance, peace, redemption from all curses, and more for our use because it's work has been completed by Jesus at the cross.

Listen to these two scriptures about the blessings <u>GOD</u> has already given believers. (Past Tense) And remember <u>GOD's word is GOD</u>. *John 1:1-3*

Ephesians 1:3 Blessed *be* <u>the God and Father of our Lord Jesus Christ</u>, who blessed us with <u>every</u> spiritual blessing in the heavenlies in Christ; Remember the Lord's prayer, "Thy will be done on earth as it is in Heaven".

Colossians 3:2 Set your minds on things that are above, not on things that are on earth.

2nd Peter 1:2-4 Grace and peace be multiplied to you through the <u>knowledge</u> of God and of Jesus our Lord, according as His divine power has given to us <u>all things</u> **that _pertain_ to life and godliness, through the <u>knowledge of Him</u>** who has called us to glory and virtue, <u>through which He has given to us exceedingly great and precious promises,</u> so that by these _Believers_ might **be partakers of _the_ divine nature**, having <u>escaped the corruption</u> _that is_ in _the_ world through lust.

To live in the Lord's divine nature, Believers must know GOD and know the blessings and promises in Heaven and earth that have been given to Believers (past tense). And remember GOD's word is GOD and His promises are yours and if you choose to be led by "GOD, the Holy Spirit" and <u>act on GOD's word</u> **you will be victorious.**

Think about this; Believers will stay in the status quo if Believers stay in their own power. <u>The Lord's Divine nature inside Believers</u> is revealed by using His promises <u>to dominate your environment, both internally and externally</u>. For Example. If you <u>do not know</u> that GOD has given you His peace and instructed Believers not to let your heart, be troubled or afraid, how are you going to capture a fearful thought, and throw it out as a lie if you <u>do not know</u> this promise?

<u>Scripture says,</u> GOD knows what you have need of before you ask and that makes sense with "GOD, the Holy Spirit" living inside you. Also, GOD supplies your needs according to His

riches in glory, how do these guarantees affect your prayer life? Or do you believe any of these promises?

Matthew 6:8 .... for <u>your Father knows what you need before you ask him.</u>

Philippians 4:19 And my God will supply every need of yours according to his riches in glory in Christ Jesus.

Hebrews 13:5 Keep your life free from love of money, and be content with what you have, for he has said, "I will never leave you nor forsake you."

If you believe GOD and His word, you can discern the thoughts and intents of your heart and control your actions by controlling your thinking. If you believe, GOD and "you are One" and nothing can separate you from the love of GOD, **your mind, and the mind of Christ inside you** will lead you into a blessed result. Now add these thoughts to the Lord's words on the new way to pray with new authority because Jesus has been to the cross and has sent Believers into the world as he was sent into the world **full of Grace and Truth and "GOD, the Holy Spirit".**

**Jesus has given Believers
a New way to Pray.**

Listen as Jesus tells Believers there is a new way to pray starting after His resurrection. <u>Wait a minute.</u> <u>Wait a minute,</u> what happened to the Lord's prayer? What is <u>the new way to pray</u> in the New Covenant? Notice the Lord's first update to the model prayer continues to start with the prayer being directed to Father GOD, but now it is offered <u>in the name of Jesus.</u>

John 16:23-24 <u>In that day</u> (after the Cross) you will ask nothing <u>of me</u>. Truly, truly, I say to you, whatever you ask of <u>the Father</u> **in my name**, he will give it to you. <u>Until now</u> you have asked nothing in my name. <u>Ask, and you will receive,</u> **that your joy may be full**.

Remember, Joy is a Fruit of your Spirit, and your Spirit is made in the exact image of GOD and will not be asking for a new car. The Lord's new way to pray is for Believers, who are "One with GOD" to ask for anything that would make their Joy full. James, the brother of Jesus, helps direct our prayer to a purpose that is not to be consumed on our lust but instead would fill us with joy.

James 4:2-3 You desire, and <u>do not have</u>. You murder, and are jealous, and cannot obtain. You fight and war, yet you have not because you ask not. <u>You ask and receive not</u>, because you ask amiss, **that you may spend *it* upon your lusts**.

Loving others more significantly than ourselves is the driving force for our lives and will assure that your prayers are always not to be consumed upon your own lusts.

Think about the situation in which Jesus lived His life under Jewish law, <u>not the grace, Jesus has given to Believers</u>. James, the brother of Jesus warns Believers to consider the purpose of our prayers. The writer of Hebrews tells Believers about the Lord's rest or peace for Believers lives if we are united with our Lord.

Hebrews 4:1-2 Therefore, while the promise of entering **his (Jesus) rest** still stands, <u>let us fear</u> lest any of you should seem to have failed to reach it. For good news came to us just as to them, but <u>the message they heard did **not** benefit them</u>, **because they were not united by faith with those who listened.**

The term "His rest" is not laying down but is resting in the faith you stand in with the Lord's promises **believing GOD has done what He said, He has done**.

What does the Bible say about effective prayers and communications with GOD.

NOW, let us do some investigation of facts around prayer and the promises of GOD.

- GOD <u>does</u> **not** answer a prayer for prosperity with money, GOD gives you the power to prosper in every area of your life as your soul prospers or as your knowledge of GOD and His promises grow in the Believers heart. (3rd John 1:2)

If you are praying for a financial need, you must expect men and women to come forth with additional business, ideas, jobs, or gifts of some kind. GOD is not going to make a deposit in your bank account. Even the manna given to Israel in the desert had to be gathered and prepared.

- GOD **will not** <u>answer</u> a prayer for something <u>that GOD has given you the authority and instruction to accomplish yourself.</u>

For example.

Let not your heart be troubled, neither let it be afraid.
Be angry and sin not.
Forgive as you have been forgiven.
Say to your mountain be removed and fall into the sea.
Cast your care on GOD for He cares for you.
Praise GOD in all things, but not for all things.

- GOD <u>will not answer</u> a prayer about <u>living under the curses</u> Believers have been redeemed from experiencing. The curses from not being able to live the law to the letter has been finished, fulfilled, and completed by Jesus. *Galatians 3:13*

For Example, here are a few curses Believers have been redeemed from experiencing:

Your land will be cursed.
Your house and food storage will be cursed.
Your womb will be cursed with few children.
Your crops will be cursed with little rain.
Your body will be inflamed and sickly.
And more. Deuteronomy 28:16-68

Believers <u>have been redeemed</u> from the curses of not living the Law to the letter, only the blessings remain for Believers.

For example, here are a few blessings for believers.

You will be blessed going in and coming out.
You will be blessed in the city and blessed in the field.
The fruit of the body will be blessed.
The fruit of your ground will be blessed.
The fruit of your cattle will be blessed.
And more. Deuteronomy 28:1-15

Are you thinking about GOD correctly?
Do you expect GOD, to want what you want?

Do you want GOD to bless **your plan** instead of asking the Almighty GOD of the Universe what His plan is for you? Think about these three reactions to problems in our daily life in a fallen world.

1. Believers turn to GOD when something bad happens, but we believe that if GOD had been there, GOD would have prevented what happened.

We assume facts not in evidence, we assume GOD allowed the calamity that happened, which is in direct opposition to GOD's promise to not tempt anyone. GOD was there waiting on Believers to act with words and actions in their authority. Listen to James the brother of Jesus.

James 1:13 Let no one <u>being tempted</u> say, I am tempted from God. For God is not tempted by evils, and <u>He tempts no one.</u>

Now a second misconception about thoughts about GOD.

2. After you believe that GOD allowed a calamity to happen to you or yours, then it does not matter if GOD intervenes to help because of reaching out to GOD with prayer or His promises, because we have already judged that GOD was not there when the calamity happened.

Again, we assume facts not in evidence, the calamity was result of a man-made plan gone bad. GOD is with Believers forever, but the power to control your environment is inside you. GOD is a Spirit and is inside you.

Hebrews 13:5 Keep your life free from love of money, and be content with what you have, for he has said, <u>"I will never leave you nor forsake you."</u>

<u>GOD was with Believers every minute waiting on Believers to take control of the situation with the power GOD has given Believers in His word.</u>

Now a third misconception about thoughts about GOD.

3. If there is no positive answer from GOD to the prayer for deliverance or a miracle for the calamity, then the people praying are sure that there is something separating them from GOD.

Again, we assume facts not in evidence, there is nothing that can separate a Believer from the love of GOD.

Romans 8:34-35 Who is to condemn? Christ Jesus is the one who died—more than that, who was raised—who is at the right hand of God, who indeed is interceding for us. Who shall separate us from the love of Christ? Shall tribulation, distress, or persecution, or famine, or nakedness, or danger, or sword? NO. Never.

Until Believers have knowledge of the authority of mankind on earth and the power of GOD's word, their incorrect thinking used in these three examples keep Believers in bondage to <u>bad thinking</u>. All acts of sin and man-made effort come from "the one act" of **not believing on** and resting in **relationship with Jesus**.

Jesus controlled his environment both physical and Spiritual with his words, thoughts, and actions, and Jesus wants Believers to do the same.

Listen, again, to the words of the New Testament and realize that these phrases are GOD's word for the direction of Believers, and they require a <u>first action</u> from the Believer <u>not from GOD</u>.

Listen for these phrases in conversation with "GOD, the Holy Spirit", as you become quiet, the Holy Spirit will speak to your mind in phrases like these phrases, for they are the "word of GOD". All these verses are words from GOD for every

Believer's life. <u>GOD has given Believers **His** authority that you may control your environment internally and externally, with your words and actions.</u>

"Seek first the kingdom of God and His righteousness
      and the needs of the world will be added."
Mathew 6:33

"Ask, seek, and knock and you shall find.
      and it shall be opened",   *Matthew 7:7*
"Spread the Gospel. Cast out devils",   *Matthew 10:7-8*
"Raise the dead, Heal the sick."   *Matthew 10:8*
"Speak to your mountain
      and cast it into the sea",   *Matthew 21:21*
"Love GOD with all your heart,
      mind, and strength".   *Mark 12:30*
"Lay hands on the sick and they shall recover", *Mark 16:18*
"Have faith in GOD",   *Mark 11:22*
"Have faith and not doubt
      what you say will come to pass"   *Mark 11:23*
"These signs shall follow
      those who believe",   *Mark 16:17*
"Love your neighbor as yourself",   *Luke 10:27*
"Believe on Him,
      whom GOD has sent",   *John 6:29*
"Let not your heart be troubled,
"Don't let it be afraid",   *John 14:1,27*
"My peace, I give you" protect it.   *John 14:27*
"Present your bodies
      as a living sacrifice",   *Romans 12:1-2*
"Do not repay evil with evil",   *Romans 12:21*
"Take every thought captive"   *2nd Corinthians 10:5*
"Abound to every good work",   *2nd Corinthians 9:8*
"Giving thanks always
      for all things unto God",   *Ephesians 5:20*
"Be strong in the Lord and

the power of His might"   *Ephesians 6:10*
"Praise Him",
"Put on the whole armor of GOD",
          Always praying in the Spirit.   *Ephesians 6:13*
"Be angry and not sin",   *Ephesians 4:26*
"Put on your new self",   *Ephesians 4:24*
"Let no corrupting talk
          come from your mouth"   *Ephesians 4:29*
"Be kind one to another",   *Ephesians 4:32*
"Forgive one another. as
          Christ has forgiven you",   *Colossians 3:13*
"Be not drunk with wine,
          but be filled with the Spirit" *Ephesians 5:18*
"Wives honor your husbands"   *Ephesians 5:22*
"Husbands love your wives,
          as Christ loves the Church" *Ephesians 5:25*
"Be found in Him",   *Philippians 3:9*
"Be anxious for nothing and
          in everything give thanks," *Philippians 4:6*
"Think on these things, whatsoever are true,
          excellent, of good report, worthy
          of praise, think on these things". *Philippians 4:8*
"Put off your old self",   *Colossians 3:9*
"Do everything in word or deed,
          do all in the name of Jesus",   *Colossians 4:17*
"Pray unceasingly",   *1ˢᵗ Thessalonians 5:17*
"Fight the good fight of faith".   *1ˢᵗ Timothy 6:12*
"Lay hold on eternal life"   *1ˢᵗ Timothy 6:12*
"Study to show yourself approved
          to GOD   *2ⁿᵈ Timothy 2:15*
"Resist the enemy and he will flee",   *James 4:7*
"Anoint the sick with oil and the prayer
          for healing will save the sick",   *James 5:8*
"Be sober minded",   *1ˢᵗ Peter 1:13*
"Cast your care on Jesus,

for He cares for you",   *1ˢᵗ Peter 5:7*
"Come boldly to the throne of grace and
          obtain mercy and find grace
              for a time of need."   *Hebrews 4:16*
"Don't love money, be content
          with what you have",   *Hebrews 13:5*

These phrases and many more scriptures call for action from the Believer, not from GOD. "GOD, the Holy Spirit" is with Believers to verify and power these actions. Listen for these words or phrases to come to your mind from "GOD, the Holy Spirit", when you pause, looking for a word from GOD for a situation. You must know the instructions and promises of GOD to put them into action. Listen to this truth from the Old Testament.

Hosea 4:6 My people are destroyed for lack of knowledge; because you have rejected knowledge, I reject you from being a priest to me. And since you have forgotten the law of your God, I also will forget your children.

Believers are no longer concerned for our salvation and future in Heaven but **lack knowledge of GOD's design systems of the world and how they operate.** This lack of knowledge has kept Believers in bondage to sickness, oppression, and demonic activity. **For Believers to succeed in this world we must understand GOD's design systems used to create the world**. The Lord's promises are added to GOD's creation design systems to counter the ravages brought about by sin. To experience the abundant life Believers must study to know what is inside your Spirit. It is very important to know what the promises are and your authority to use them, because Believers have dominion over everything on the earth, above the earth, and under the earth if you believe GOD.

Genesis 1:26-29 And God said, Let us make man in our image, after our likeness: and **let them have dominion** over the fish of the sea, and over the fowl of the air, and over the cattle, and over all the earth, and over every creeping thing that creeps upon the earth. So God created man in his *own* image, in the image of God created he him; male and female created he them. **And God blessed them**, and God said unto them, Be fruitful, and multiply, and replenish the earth, and **subdue it**: and **have dominion** over the fish of the sea, and over the fowl of the air, and over every living thing that moves upon the earth.

Now, let us look at a design system the Lord's model prayer for insights into how to approach prayer and communicating with GOD **after Jesus had been resurrected** and <u>given Believers His authority on earth</u>.

**The Lord's model Prayer
given <u>before</u> Jesus had gone to the cross.**

The Lord's model prayer can be summarized like this:

Dedication to Father God and praise for who GOD is.
Alignment with GOD's will in Heaven,
      for your life and will on earth.
Provision requests daily.
Pardon request.
Protection request.
I add, "for yours is the Kingdom and the Power and the Glory forever." Amen. This ending is not in the original text, but it really helps the song when we sing it. Laugh Ha! The ending is also in the Old Testament version of a Model Prayer, *1ˢᵗ Chronicles 29:11*.

Notice, that the Model or Lord's prayer is not requested in "The Name and power of Jesus" because Jesus had not been to the cross.

**The reason to pray and talk to GOD,
is to align our will on Earth
with our Father's will in Heaven.**

Jesus' lesson on prayer starts with what **not to say** and **do**.

Matthew 6:5 "And when you pray, you must <u>not</u> be like the hypocrites. For they love to stand and pray in the synagogues and at the street corners, that they may be seen by others. Truly, I say to you, <u>they have received their reward.</u>

Jesus tells Believes to <u>pray to our Father</u>, not Jesus, not His mama, but **our unseen Father.**

Matthew 6:6 But when you pray, <u>go into your room and shut the door</u> and pray to <u>your Father</u> who is in secret. **And <u>your Father</u> who sees in secret <u>will reward you.</u>**

Matthew 6:7-9 "And <u>when you pray</u>, do not heap up empty phrases as the Gentiles do, for they think that they will be heard for their many words. Do not be like them, <u>for your Father knows what you need before you ask him.</u>

If GOD already knows our needs, what do we need to do with our prayer? **Answer**, prayer, and our constant conversation with GOD brings the Believer close to GOD, it slows Believers down, and makes time for Believers thoughts **to align our will with GOD's will**. At a time of anxiety, think about who God is and unload what is bothering you on GOD, with the freedom of knowing GOD is carrying your load. Then, listen to GOD's leadership.

The Apostle Peter tells us to "Cast your care (anxiety) on GOD, for GOD cares (His promises eradicate problems) for you" *1ˢᵗ Peter 5:7*

In the next verse of the model prayer, Jesus is telling us to relate to the Spiritual Creator of All, as the perfect Father.

Pray then like this: **"Our Father in heaven, hallowed be your name.**

The Lord is offering time, to stop and see the perfect Father who cares about His child, the child who has come to talk to their Dad in a personal private meeting.

Your Kingdom come, your will be done, on earth as it is in Heaven.

The purpose of prayer and conversation with "GOD, the Holy Spirit" is to **reposition ourselves to GOD's purpose** or to **find GOD's will for our moment or day**. God wants us to surrender our will to take up a GOD blessed plan or direction for each new moment in our life.

What is your view of GOD? Are you using GOD like an ATM? Or Conscience cleaner? Or Santa Claus? How is that working?

Prayer and conversation with GOD are recognizing and surrendering to the Father's will for a plan that will avoid the circumstances that generally caused you to come to GOD in prayer.

Give us this day our daily bread.

This request brings Believers into the position of depending on GOD for all our needs including a word or plan for the day.

And forgive me for my sins as I forgive those who have sins against me.

Do not think that prayer is a conscience cleaner. Keeping resentment, revenge, and anger in our hearts is **to not follow** what our heavenly Father wants for us. **Unforgiveness hurts Believers** and keeps Believers from proper thinking.

And lead us not into temptation, but deliver us from evil.

To ask to be led is to agree to FOLLOW GOD. Are you ready to follow Jesus?

Then Jesus told his disciples, "If anyone would come after me, let him deny himself and take up his cross and follow me.

Do not ask, "Why am I here?" But ask, "**Who am I here for**?" GOD will lead you to do for others what GOD has done for you.

Lord's Prayer or Model Prayer
After Jesus had gone to the Cross.

The following discussion of the Lord's model prayer is **not** an attempt to change the model prayer or the Bible but to give **a new picture of prayer** to the Church. The redemption of mankind including GOD's gift of part of Himself, to abide in every Believer, in "GOD, the Holy Spirit" and to see Jesus elevated to the right hand of GOD as the Believer's advocate and High Priest has changed the world. The devil is no longer able to accuse the Believers in the presence of GOD, because Jesus is at GOD's right hand.

Here are some of the plausible additions to the model prayer for Believers after receiving the inheritance of Jesus Christ's after His death. What do you think it means to Believers to have an advocate for Believers sitting next to Father GOD?

> _Matthew 6:9_ **Pray then like this: "Our Father in heaven, hallowed be your name.**

Now Jesus is in Heaven with Father GOD and "GOD, the Holy Spirit" is on earth with Believers.

> _Matthew 6:10_ **Your kingdom come, your will be done, on earth as it is in heaven.**

Now the "Kingdom of GOD" has come to the hearts of Believers as it is in Heaven and GOD's will is being done, on earth, one heart at a time.

> _Matthew 6:11_ **Give us this day our daily bread,**

GOD's word is our daily bread and His promises our provision.

> _Matthew 6:12_ **and forgive us our debts, as we also have forgiven our debtors.**

GOD has forgiven Believers every sin so Believers can forgive others for anything suffered by the Believer.

> _Matthew 6:13_ **And lead us not into temptation, but deliver us from evil.**

Thank you Jesus, that greater is **"GOD, the Holy Spirit" in Believers**, than the devil's influence in the world.

Putting these changes together, an update to the Lord's model prayer, after His ascension to Heaven and the giving of "GOD, the Holy Spirit" might sound like this:

**Model prayer for the New Covenant
after the Lord's sacrifice.**

Pray like this; **Our Father GOD and Jesus Christ, our Redeemer, which art in Heaven and "GOD, the Holy Spirit" abiding with Believers on earth, hallowed be your name.**

Father, your Kingdom has come into the hearts of Believers and your will is being done, in those who believe in Jesus Christ as Redeemer, as it is in Heaven.

Thank you for making provision for my daily needs at creation, at redemption, and through "GOD, the Holy Spirit" by faith.

Thank you for forgiving and forgetting my sin so that I might forgive others and never walk-in condemnation for the sin you have forgotten.

I praise you Father for sending "GOD, the Holy Spirit" to guide my steps, to teach me all things, and to tell me of things to come, that I may become a light to the world and bring glory to my Redeemer and praise to the glory of The Father.

Praise you Father that "GOD, the Holy Spirit" is inside me and is more powerful than any evil influence in the world, and I dedicate my service to honoring GOD and others more significantly than to myself that you may receive glory. And I pray this in the name of Jesus, my Savior.

For you Father, have established Jesus over your Kingdom in the hearts of Believers, for ever and ever. Amen and Amen.

This prayer shows the model prayer considering <u>Jesus going to the cross and reconciling Believers to GOD and the sending of</u> "GOD, the Holy Spirit" to Believers.

Conclusion from the Apostle Paul talking to the Church at Philippi about living the "Worship lifestyle".

The Lord is at hand; <u>do not be anxious about anything,</u> but in everything <u>by prayer</u> and <u>supplication</u> **with thanksgiving** let your requests be made known to God. And **the peace of God**, which surpasses all understanding, <u>will guard your hearts and your minds in Christ Jesus.</u> *Philippians 4:6-7*

This is another scripture moving Believers from a prayer, for a list of needs, to talking to GOD all day in a lifestyle of worship, love, and service to Almighty GOD.

Chapter 7

Understanding the word "sin".
Death by Adam, or Life in Christ.

The word sin, used in the Bible, is a confusing word because it encompasses some physical acts of performance (lawlessness or morality) or some spiritual acts of the free-will (Covenant breaking) both having different penalties and the difference <u>between the sin of bad acts</u> and the sin of **not** having a Savior in your life, is larger than the divide in the Grand Canyon. The sin of bad acts or lawlessness is a horizontal act of performance, only on the earth, that can be forgiven with GOD's mercy, <u>but rejection of Jesus Christ and GOD, results in a vertical separation from GOD, stretching up to eternity and covenant breaking must be redeemed</u> rather than forgiven.

The breaking Covenant by Adam and Eve corrupted and caused their spirit to die and the seed of the First Adam to be corrupted. This corrupted seed was inherited by all of mankind born from the line of Adam and Eve. **Jesus had to re-purchase or redeem right standing with GOD** <u>and conquer death and the grave, by becoming a new seed, so mankind could be born-again from the Seed of Jesus and fellowship with GOD, again.</u>

Note, Adam and Eve broke covenant with GOD, it is often called sin, but they lived before "the law" that had a consequence of sin. Without the law there is no sin added to a person's account, and the law did not come into being for thousands of years. Breaking Covenant with GOD is much worse than sin of bad acts and had automatic consequences.

<u>*Romans 4:15*</u> …, for where no law is, *there is* no transgression.

Romans 5:13 for until the Law sin was in *the* world, but sin is not imputed *when* there is no law.

*Adam was created **with the nature of GOD, in his Spirit**, and given dominion on the earth. When Adam spoke, the things on earth obeyed the content of Adam's words. After Adam broke covenant with GOD, every person ever born, is born with a nature to sin, without GOD's glory, and without knowledge of Believer's dominion over GOD's designed world systems.*

*After being Born-again, Believers are reconciled to GOD or, said another way, Believers are in right-standing with GOD, and Believers have been given a New Spirit, with the nature of GOD in your New Spirit and dominion over GOD's World's systems. **Unfortunately, the new Believer's mind is not renewed and therefore the power over your environment starts with your current knowledge of GOD, His world systems, and the knowledge of your inheritance as a child of GOD.** Without knowledge of GOD's word to dominate the world systems using the Believers faith filled words, the Believer must operate at the level of what they know. Think about and listen to the words of Jesus to the two blind men.*

Matthew 9:28-30 And when He had come into the house, the blind men came to Him. And Jesus said to them, "Do you believe that I am able to do this?" They said to Him, "Yes, Lord". Then He touched their eyes, saying, according to your faith let it be to you. And their eyes were opened.

Believers must believe, Jesus has completed the prophecies of the Old Testament, and the Godhead is waiting on Believers to appropriate the promises, Jesus authorized Believers to use.

Mankind did nothing to deserve to be born a sinner and Believers did nothing

to deserve to be <u>made righteous.</u>

Listen to the Apostle Paul confirm it is <u>not</u> the fault of mankind, they are born with a "nature to sin" instead of the "nature of GOD".

Romans 5:12 Therefore, even as through one man (*Adam broke covenant with GOD*) sin entered into the world, and death by sin, and so death (a sin-nature) passed on to all men in as much as all inherited a "sin nature". (B*orn with a sin-nature, possessing the knowledge of good and evil*).

Notice in this next verse, that sin of lawlessness (horizontal or worldly sin) was not accounted to mankind's account until Moses was given the law, these sins are not a covenant busting sin but a horizontal performance sin of lust of the flesh, lust of the eye, and pride of one's life that results in man-made results or consequences.

Romans 5:13-14 for until the Law sin was in *the* world, <u>but sin is not imputed *when* there is no law</u>. But death reigned from Adam to Moses, even over those who had not sinned <u>in the likeness</u> of the <u>transgression of Adam, who is the type of Jesus</u> who was to come;

Now listen closely as the Apostle Paul explains, with three repeats, <u>that man did not cause himself to be a sinner</u>, Mankind was born with a sin-nature because Adam and Eve could no longer pass on to their children their original "nature of GOD", for they had corrupted it with their free-will. And now for the most difficult concept in the Church! Mankind did NOTHING and CAN DO NOTHING to buy, earn, or deserve mankind's "right standing" with GOD, <u>it is a gift from a loving</u>

GOD for belief in Jesus Christ, the second Adam or the last Adam.

Life with Jesus is not behavioral modification but is Spiritual transformation. Any sin-consciousness behavior by Believers is wrong and any motivation to work for GOD's acceptance, or to deserve answered prayer, or other benefit of salvation is misplaced; if you think that you are entitled that is failed thinking. The benefits of Salvation are "done" a fact, completed, finished, and are an inheritance for Believers: you have been saved, you have been healed, you have been delivered, you have been sanctified. GOD loves Believers without respect to their horizontal performance on earth. GOD loves you because GOD is Love, not because you are lovable.

Now, the Apostle Paul repeats several times in Romans 5 the offense of Adam brings death. **Choosing Jesus Christ brings life eternal or reconciliation with GOD.** *ALERT! A Believers' bad acts are not counted against the Believer because Believers are not under the law, but bad actions have consequences within themselves. (If you overeat you will get fat. If you murder, you will go to prison.)*

<u>Romans 5:15</u> but the free gift (salvation) *shall* not *be* also like the offense. For if by the offense of the one (*Adam*) many died, much more the grace of God, and the **gift in grace**; which *is* of the one Man, Jesus Christ, abounded to many.

Second repeat.

<u>Romans 5:16</u> And the free gift *shall* not *be* as by one (*Adam*) having sinned *(or broken Covenant)*; (for indeed the judgment *(of Adam) was* of one to condemnation, but the free gift (of Jesus) *is* of many offenses to justification.

Third repeat.

Romans 5:17 For if by one man's offense death reigned by one (*Adam*), much more they who receive abundance of grace and the gift of righteousness shall reign in life by One, Jesus Christ.

Mankind did nothing to deserve to be born a sinner and Believer's did nothing to deserve to be made righteous, **but your Spirit is made righteous if you have been born-again and accepted the free gift of righteousness from Jesus Christ.** Believers must know that Believers are freed from the sin-nature. Listen to the Apostle Paul.

Romans 6:6 knowing this, that our old man is crucified with *Him* in order that the body of sin might be destroyed, that from now on we should **not serve sin**.

Believers must know their "sin-nature" has been crucified (past tense) with Jesus at the cross and **there is no condemnation** to Believers *from GOD*. Believers are freed from their "sin nature"; not free to sin.

Receiving GOD's grace does not give Christians a license to sin; everyone has been sinning without a license since birth. The Believers New Spirit is a gift that cannot be earned or deserved by performance but by believing and receiving GOD's grace gives Christians a new "Nature of GOD" and believing in what "Jesus has done" allows Believers to live right and blessed through believing right and acting in love for the people GOD loves.

The motivation for living right out of behavior modification in the Believer's own strength will result in man-made results without GOD's blessing. **Christians have been sent into the world, as Jesus was sent into the world filled with "GOD,**

the Holy Spirit", to bring the light of life in Christ Jesus to all who will believe. Listen to this guidance from the Apostle Paul to live right and do good. Treating your brothers and sisters of the world with the love you have received from GOD is the only way to live and **honor GOD**.

Titus 2:11-14 For the grace of God has appeared, bringing salvation for all people, **training us** to renounce ungodliness and worldly passions, and to live self-controlled, upright, and godly lives in the present age, waiting for our blessed hope, the appearing of the glory of our great God and Savior Jesus Christ, who gave himself for us to redeem us from all lawlessness and to purify for himself a people for **his own possession** who are zealous for good works.

GOD does not see you the way that you are, GOD sees you **the way GOD's word says you are. Look at the table showing a vertical axis and a horizontal axis with GOD's preferred ends.**

A vertical "born-again" relationship with GOD through Jesus Christ with eternal life at the top.

Or on the lower end of the vertical axis, living for yourself, rejecting GOD and His Son, resulting in death and permanent separation from GOD.

The horizontal plane reflects performance during life on Earth: Man-made performance or GOD inspired performance. This line reflects your performance from selfish to totally giving. Living for yourself or living in Jesus and for GOD with God's design of the world systems working for you.

BELIEF

Born-again with the

Nature of GOD

With motivation to

Live for Jesus and have

Eternal Life through grace

+

+

BEHAVIOR	+	**Living in the Spirit**
Man-made Systems	+	GOD's World Systems
Acts of evil	+	Acts of Kindness
Works of the flesh	−	Fruit of the Spirit
Influenced by the devil	−	Led by Holy Spirit
Living under the law	−	Circle of Grace

−

Sin-nature from Adam

Eternal Death

Nature to sin

Motivated to live for yourself.

and reject Jesus as Savior.

<u>Think about sin from two perspectives.</u>

<u>The acts of an unbeliever</u> ~~can~~ get nothing from GOD and His World Systems until the **un**believer chooses to want GOD in their life through Jesus Christ's redemption of mankind.

<u>The Believer's acts of kindness</u> and application of the Fruit of the Spirit to live the abundant life with Jesus Christ, stores up treasure in Heaven and is a blessed way to live.

**The sin and penalty <u>for all sin</u> has been paid.
Jesus recorded the name of everyone who has lived
or will live in the "Lamb's book of Life".**

<u>Remember</u> Jesus died for <u>everyone who has ever lived</u>, and Jesus wrote every name of everyone who has ever lived or will live in the "Lamb's Book of Life", **rejection of Jesus as Lord will cause a name to be blotted out of the "Lamb's Book of Life"**. <u>GOD's desire</u> is for everyone to be saved but <u>not all will</u> <u>choose Jesus, as Lord</u>, **with their free-will**. Listen to these scriptures.

Revelation 3:5 (Jesus speaking) The one who conquers will be clothed thus in white garments, and **<u>I will never blot his name out</u> of the book of Life**. <u>I will confess his name before my</u> <u>Father and before his angels.</u>

Revelation 21:22-27 And I saw no temple in the city, for its temple is the Lord God the Almighty and the Lamb. And the city has no need of sun or moon to shine on it, for the glory of God gives it light, and its lamp is the Lamb. By its light will the nations walk, and the kings of the earth will bring their glory into it, and its gates will never be shut by day—and there will be no night there. They will bring into it the glory and the honor of the nations. But nothing unclean will ever enter it, nor anyone who does what is detestable or false, **but only those who are written in the Lamb's book of life**. 122

Note. The Lord's sacrifice for sin and receipt of the penalty of GOD's wrath for the entire universe of sin for every person who has or will live, has been accepted as "paid in full". The Lord's sacrifice and receipt of the wrath of GOD <u>paid the penalty for all sin</u>. **Every person who has ever lived <u>has no sin in their account</u> but to be Born-again and be given a New Spirit made in the image of GOD is reserved for <u>those who believe and call on the Name of Jesus Christ as Savior.</u> This belief in Jesus, as Savior, triggers Jesus to exchange His Righteousness to your account and give the Believer a New Spirit made in the exact image of GOD.**

Now let us look at the power of the Gospel of Jesus Christ or "the Gospel". The word "Gospel" used by Jesus and the Apostle Paul is considerably grander in scope and power than its use today. When Jesus testified of the Gospel of the Kingdom or the Gospel of the Kingdom of Heaven: <u>Jesus was telling the Jews and Gentiles</u> that <u>the prophesied coming of the Messiah,</u> <u>had come,</u> and was on Earth to deliver everyone from <u>death,</u> the <u>oppression of the devil,</u> the <u>curse of the law,</u> and to restore the glory of GOD to all of Abraham's descendants who believe. Listen to the Apostle Paul testify of the Gospel of Jesus Christ.

<u>*Romans 1:16-17*</u> For I am <u>not</u> ashamed of the gospel, for it is the power of God for salvation to everyone who believes, to the Jew first and also to the Greek. For in it the righteousness of God is revealed from faith to faith, as it is written, "The righteous (or justified) shall live by faith."

The Apostle Paul knew, "He was blinded and now he sees", he was a murderer and now he was made righteous by Jesus Christ, <u>not because of his performance</u> but **by faith in the performance of Jesus, as Savior.**

The GOSPEL is, the coming of the Messiah, the reversing of the penalty of sin, sickness, oppression, and separation from GOD. To Believers, Jesus returned the authority to reign on earth, Jesus restored GOD's glory to Believers, and gave the gift of "GOD, the Holy Spirit" to live inside Believers. And all this, so Believers could give GOD's love to their neighbor, and to the world, and be seen as the praise of GOD's glory.

**The motivation to live right,
should come from love and service to GOD.**

You have heard the expression, "hurt people hurt people". Well, **"Godly people do people good"**. If you think about all the instructions of the Lord and the Apostle Paul, they revolve around a motivation **to <u>never</u> hurt people**.

Don't commit adultery, **<u>not</u> <u>because it is wrong</u>, but because it hurts people** and <u>GOD loves people</u>.

Don't steal, **<u>not</u> <u>because it's wrong,</u> but because it hurts people** and <u>GOD loves people</u>.

Don't murder, **<u>not</u> <u>because it is wrong</u>, but because it hurts people** and <u>GOD loves people</u>.

Don't lie, gossip, lust, steal, etc. **because it hurts people** and <u>GOD loves people</u>.

GOD loves people and Believers need to love people also.

Chapter 8

**Jesus gave Believers the "Shall not promises".
The keys to living in the Spirit of Christ and
Operating in the "Circle of grace".**

How do Believers partake of the Spiritual life, Jesus has given Believers? First, have confidence in "who you are" because of "who Jesus is". Jesus, is the Good Shepherd and has set a table for Believers in the presence of our enemies, the menu includes: living bread, water for thirst, light for life, peace that Believers will never perish, freedom from condemnation, everlasting life, His personal presence, never to be forsaken, and never to be ashamed; your cup is overflowing and your head has been anointed with oil from "GOD the Holy Spirit". It is a love feast for your new heart, eat and drink to your hearts content with your host, Jesus Christ.

Whoever believes in Him **shall not perish** and
  have everlasting life. *John 3:16*

Whoever drinks of this water, that I shall give,
  shall never thirst. *John 4:14*

I am the bread of life: he that comes to me,
  shall never hunger. *John 6:36*

Whoever hears my word and believes on <u>him</u>
  <u>who sent me</u> has eternal life.
  He **shall not come into judgment**, *John 5:24*

I am the light of the world, <u>He that follows me</u>,
  shall not walk in darkness
  but <u>shall have the light of life</u>. *John 8:12*

I give them eternal life: and <u>no one</u>
      will snatch them out of my hand
      and they **<u>shall never perish</u>**.   *John 10:28*

I am the resurrection and the life:
      he that believes in me,
      <u>though He were dead</u>,
      yet shall He live and whosoever believes.
      in me **<u>shall never die</u>**.   *John 11:25-26*

"Behold, a chief corner Stone, elect, precious,
      and <u>he who believes on Him</u>
      <u>shall never be ashamed</u>."   *1st Peter 2:6*

<u>Keep your life free from love of money</u>, and
      be content with what you have,
      for he (Jesus) has said, "**I will <u>never</u>**
      <u>leave you</u> nor forsake you."   *Hebrews 13:5*

Jesus is using the negative "**shall not or never**" to assure Believers of their "eternal" relationship with GOD is to be experienced on earth, in the Millennium, and in Heaven. **Now listen** As John, the Apostle, uses these thoughts in the positive or affirmative form confirming the availability of an "eternal" relationship with GOD right now, and Christ living in you.

**Eternal life with Jesus Christ,
starts at Salvation, right now on earth.**

GOD made the earth to have a place to have a relationship with His created people and GOD does not want to wait until Heaven to have a relationship with you. If Heaven was the end all, GOD could have skipped creating the earth. **Eternal life starts at Salvation, so GOD can be with you, now**.

Listen to these scriptures verify eternal life starting at salvation, just in the book of John. (There are many more in the other gospels.)

John 3:14-15 And as Moses lifted up the serpent in the wilderness, so must the Son of Man be lifted up, that whoever believes in him **may have eternal life.**

John 3:16 "For God so loved the world, that he gave his only Son, that whoever believes in him **should not perish** but **have eternal life.**

John 3:36 Whoever believes in the Son **has eternal life**; whoever does not obey the Son **shall not** **see life**, but the wrath of God remains on him.

John 4:14 but whoever drinks the water that I will give him **will never be thirsty again**. The water that I will give him will become in him a spring of water welling up **to eternal life.**"

John 5:24 Truly, truly, I say to you, He who hears My Word and believes on Him who sent Me **has everlasting life** and shall not come into condemnation, but has passed from death to life.

John 5:25 Truly, truly, I say to you, the hour is coming and now is, when the dead shall hear the voice of the Son of God, and **they who hear shall live.**

John 6:27 Do not work for the food that perishes, but for the food that **endures to eternal life**, which the Son of Man will give to you. For on him God the Father has set his seal."

John 6:40 For this is <u>the will of my Father</u>, that everyone <u>who looks on the Son and believes in him</u> should **have eternal life**, and I will raise him up on the last day."

John 12:49-50 For I have not spoken on my own authority, <u>but the Father who sent me</u> has himself given me a commandment—what to say and what to speak. And I know that <u>his commandment</u> **is eternal life.** What I say, therefore, **I say as the Father has told me.**"

John 17:3 And **this is life eternal**, that they might <u>know You</u>, **the only true God**, and **Jesus Christ** whom **You have sent.**

What a blessing to know that Believers can be "One with GOD" right now, if you <u>believe GOD</u>, and <u>His word</u>, and not just believe <u>in a</u> GOD.

Be Alive in Christ, because Christ is alive in you,
And take the next right step.

The Apostle Paul gives Believers daily marching orders: **walk in Him, be rooted in Him, be built up in Him, be established in the Gospel of Good news, and abound in thanksgiving.** Do not be misled by any philosophy that does not measure up to the truth of Christ Jesus: <u>love GOD</u>, <u>love your brothers in Christ</u>, and <u>love your neighbors as you love yourself</u>. Listen as the Apostle Paul explains living In Christ with all the <u>in Him</u> phrases, so you will know Christ is living in you.

Colossians 2:6-15 Therefore, as you received Christ Jesus the Lord, so **walk <u>in him</u>, rooted, and built up <u>in him</u>** and established in the faith, <u>just as you were taught</u>, abounding in thanksgiving.

See to it that no one takes you captive by philosophy and empty deceit, according to human tradition, according to the elemental spirits of the world, and **<u>not</u> according to Christ**.

For <u>in him</u> (Jesus) the whole fullness of GOD dwells bodily, and you have been filled <u>in him,</u> who is the head of all rule and authority. **<u>In him</u>** also you were circumcised with a circumcision made <u>without</u> hands, by putting off the body of the flesh, by the circumcision of Christ, (a circumcision of the heart) having been buried **<u>with him</u>** in baptism, in which you were also raised **<u>with him</u>** through faith in the powerful working of "God, the Holy Spirit" who raised Jesus from the dead.

And you, <u>who were dead</u> in your trespasses and the uncircumcision of your flesh, <u>God made alive</u> together **<u>with Him (Jesus)</u>**, <u>having</u> <u>forgiven us all our trespasses</u>, by canceling the record of debt that stood against us with its legal demands. This he (Jesus) set aside, **nailing it to the cross**.

He (Jesus) disarmed the rulers and authorities and put them to open shame, by **triumphing over them <u>in him</u>**.

Romans 5:2-5 **Through Him** we also have <u>access by faith (Undeserved Privilege) into this grace</u> in which we stand, and we rejoice on the hope of the glory of God. And not only *this*, but we glory in afflictions (or weakness) also, knowing that afflictions work out patience, and patience *works out* experience, and experience *works out* hope and hope <u>does not</u> put us to shame, because God's love has been poured into our hearts through the Holy Spirit who has been given to us.

The Apostle Paul is so eloquent in his description "Eternal Life" with Jesus living in Believers and living through "GOD, the Holy Spirit" with his use of <u>Believers living **"in Him"**</u>. Now let us look further into Grace, that is Jesus Christ, not only for Salvation but also for times of need during our time as Ambassador for the Kingdom of GOD.

Section 2. Let us **investigate the "Undeserved Privilege" of this grace** in which we stand, GOD's sufficiency during a time of our weakness to accomplish **loving others as Jesus has loved us.**

There is a "Grace" for being a Believer
and "Grace" for stewarding GOD's abundance.

In a time of need, when Believers are facing an issue and realize the weakness in our own power, we must return to the "Throne of Grace" for revelation of GOD's grace, power, or supply to **replace** our weakness with **GOD's sufficiency**. This is the circle of grace and a wonderful way to live having **Christ living through Believers**.

Stewarding GOD's abundance on Earth is the Believers destiny, and often requires more grace or supply than Believers have. Believers in times of weakness have a back-up.

Hebrews 4:16 Believers come boldly to the "Throne of Grace" to obtain mercy and **find grace** for their time of need.

Finding grace for each day is the Believers realization that GOD's plan for their day is greater than their ability can handle. It is then that the Believer superimposes GOD's strength for their weakness for their time of need.

Jesus and Father GOD welcome

Believers to come "boldly" to **the Throne of Grace**

Where Jesus, stands as a Father, husband,

and brother, and **with Him,**

Believers will receive power and supply,

since it is kept **for Him, by Him and with Him,**

and is only dispensed **through Him,**

and **in Him** we know grace,

Since all the fulness of grace dwells **in Him.**

In times of world calamities finding help is laid on GOD inside us. Coming to the throne of Grace in a time of need is normal.

Help for GOD's plan in your weakness, to be One with GOD

in His plan's completion. All of God is with Believers

in stewarding GOD's abundance,

for Christ is the Believers sufficiency

for acts of kindness. And it is by Him

that the Saints glory in our weakness, To show His majesty.

And each trip to the Throne of Grace, Excitement grows.

To do what we cannot do

without being "One with Christ".

Hebrews 4:15-16 For we do not have a high priest who cannot be touched with the feelings of our infirmities but was in all points tempted just as *we are, yet* without sin. **Therefore, let us come boldly to the throne of grace,** that we may obtain mercy and find grace to help **in times of need**.

Notice. The power of GOD is available to Believers when we are tempted, just as it was to Jesus, "GOD, the Holy Spirit" was with Jesus and is with Believers and the Throne of Grace is open 24/7.

**Quit thinking "You are only human"!
Your Spirit is made in the exact image of Jesus Christ.
And you have the Mind of Christ in your Spirit.**

A Believer is "<u>not</u>" only human but is mighty through GOD, whose Spirit is born-again and is eternal. When a Believer abides with GOD, receives motivation from His or Her "Oneness with GOD", and is constantly in communication with "GOD, the Holy Spirit" **nothing is impossible**.

Ephesians 2:8-9 For by grace you are saved through faith, and that not of yourselves, *it is* <u>the gift of God</u>, not of works, lest <u>anyone should boast</u>. **For we are *His* workmanship, created in Christ Jesus to good works, which God has before ordained that we should walk in them**.

Notice, we are <u>His workmanship</u> from the <u>incorruptible seed of His Son</u>, who is <u>the word of GOD</u> made flesh. Just as we are New Creations through GOD's word, <u>our New Spirit is made in the exact image of GOD</u>. Listen to the beauty of this next scripture from the Apostle Peter and realize who you are in Christ Jesus.

1st Peter 1:22-25 Purifying your souls in the obedience of the truth <u>through the Spirit</u> to <u>unfeigned love of the brothers</u>, <u>love one another fervently out of a pure heart</u>, having been born again, **not of corruptible seed**, <u>but of incorruptible, through the "living Word" of God, and "abiding forever"</u>.

For all flesh *is* as grass, and all the glory of men as the flower of the grass. The grass withers, and its flower falls out, **but the Word of the Lord endures forever**. And this is the Word preached as gospel to you.

Notice, the contrast between an eternal Spirit and flesh, the flesh dies. It is only the Believer's Spirit birthed from the word of GOD, that **remains forever**. In the flesh, everyone is born selfish and must be taught to share and love others.

Think about this first, without qualification, Believers were included in GOD's family, Father GOD gave His son and Jesus gave his life and "GOD, the Holy Spirit" is given to Believers. Now would be the right time for Believers to love GOD in return.

Section 2.

GOD's Kingdom is inside Believers right now.

Colossians 1:9-14 For this cause we also, since the day we heard, do not cease to pray for you, and to desire that you might be filled *with* the knowledge of His will in all wisdom and spiritual understanding, that you might walk worthy of the Lord to all pleasing, being fruitful in every work and **increasing in the knowledge of God**,

being empowered with all power, according to the might of His glory, to all patience and long-suffering with joyfulness, giving thanks to the Father, who has made us meet to be partakers of the inheritance of the saints in light. *For He* has **delivered us from the power of darkness** and has **translated** *us* **into the kingdom of His dear Son**; in whom we have redemption through His blood, the remission of sins.

Think about the words from the Lord's prayer, "Thy kingdom come", it does not say, "Believers will go". The Kingdom of GOD's dear Son **is now born in our Spirits on earth.**

Then Father GOD sent **HIS Holy Spirit** to inhabit the Spiritual Kingdom in every Believer's New heart or Spirit. Listen to the words of Jesus.

John 16:13-15 When the **Spirit of truth** comes, he will guide you into all the truth, (Jesus is Grace and truth) for he will not speak on his own authority, but whatever he hears he will speak, and he will declare to you **the things that are to come**. He will glorify me, for he will take what is mine and **declare it to you**. All that the Father has is mine; therefore, I said that he will take what is mine and declare it to you.

For those who are beaten down and do not seem to be hearing from GOD or receiving motivation for your day from His word, the next scriptures may give a new hope. Believers do not have to depend on their faith but instead can depend on the "Lord's faith", it is Him, **Jesus Christ whose finished works are the Lord's promises by which we have authority in the earth to dominate our environment. Have faith in His faith.**

Keep in Step with your Spirit, and
you will **not** fall prey to acting out of emotions.

Know this; love, joy, peace, faith, gentleness, goodness, temperance, and self-control are yours and, in your Spirit, and available to thwart any thought of the flesh, and are backed up with the power of "GOD, the Holy Spirit".

Galatians 5:16-25 But I say, **walk by the Spirit**, and you will not gratify the desires of the flesh. For the desires of the flesh are against the Spirit, and **the desires of the Spirit are against**

the flesh, for these (the desires of the flesh) are opposed to each other, <u>to keep you from doing the things you want to do</u>. But **if you are led by the Spirit**, you are not under the law (and can do what you are lead to do). And now listen to the next scripture.

**The Believer's Spirit is filled,
with GOD's way for living.**

Galatians 5:22-25 But **the fruit of the Spirit** is love, joy, peace, patience, kindness, goodness, faith, gentleness, and self-control; against such things there is no law. And <u>those who belong to Christ Jesus have crucified the flesh with its passions and desires</u>. If we live by the Spirit, <u>let us also keep in step with the Spirit</u>.

Focus on GOD and the Spiritual realm
and not the flesh.

Isaiah 26:2-4 Open the gates, that the righteous nation that keeps faith may enter in. You **(GOD) keeps him in perfect peace** <u>whose **mind is stayed on you**, because he trusts in you</u>. Trust in the LORD forever, for the LORD GOD is an everlasting rock.

**Magnify your eternal solution
and minimize time and challenges on earth.**

2nd Corinthians 4:16-18 Though our outer self (Body) is wasting away, <u>our inner self is being renewed day by day</u>. For

135

this light momentary affliction (aging of our Body and time on earth) is preparing for us an eternal weight of glory **beyond all comparison**, as we look not to the things that are seen but to the things that are unseen. For the things that are seen are transient, but the things that are unseen are eternal.

**Let your light shine before men,
Through good works that glorify GOD.**

Matthew 5:16 Let your light so shine before men, that they may see your good works, and glorify your Father which is in heaven.

Follow GOD's will to victory.

John 5:30 "I can do nothing on my own. As I hear, I judge, and my judgment is just because I seek not my own will but the will of him who sent me.

Conclusion

Jesus went about doing good and healing all who were oppressed of the Devil. It is our goal to do likewise and if we come up against a strong enemy we can turn to the Throne of Grace and find grace for our time of need and accomplish the act of kindness we were given. Believers are not just human **but mighty through GOD.** *Acts 10:38*

Section 3.

**Your Spirit is made in the image of GOD,
And knows <u>all things.</u>**

The Apostle Peter tells us that <u>there is information already inside Believers. Imagine what intellect, information, and power is in the Spirit made in the image of GOD, inside Believers</u>. The "Born-again Spirit" given to Believers is a full grown, eternal Spirit made in the image of GOD. This fact forms the basis for asking "GOD, the Holy Spirit" for direction and allowing the peace of GOD to rule over your thoughts and actions. Listen to this word from Peter.

1st Peter 1:13-16 Therefore, <u>preparing your minds for action,</u> and <u>being sober-minded,</u> set your hope fully on the grace that will be brought to you **at the revelation of Jesus Christ**. As obedient children, <u>do not be conformed</u> to the passions of your former ignorance, but as he who called you is holy (separated from the physical world), you also be holy (separated from the fleshly desires of the world.) in all your conduct, since it is written, "You shall be holy, for I am holy."

Note, the word Holy, used here is "<u>separated from the systems of the flesh</u> and **dedicated to GOD**" as GOD is separated to you. In other scriptures, "live in the Spiritual realm because GOD is Spirit" and "put off the old man and put on the new man".

**Jesus "is" coming again.
<u>Not to deal with sin</u>, but to pick up His Bride.**

Believers have heard the words of Eternal Life and received the guarantee of the presence of "GOD, the Holy Spirit" inside each Believer to experience eternal life, **daily with GOD**. Death of the body will release the Believer from dependance on Earth for physical life (blood, water, air, and food), to the Spirit realm with your "Eternal" family.

Hebrews 9:27-28 And just as it is appointed for man to die once, and after that comes judgment, so Christ, having been offered once to bear the sins of many, will appear a second time, **not to deal with sin** but to save those who are eagerly waiting for him (Believers).

Hebrews 2:14-15 Since then the children have partaken of flesh and blood, He also Himself likewise partook of the same; that through death He might destroy him who had the power of death (that is, the Devil), and deliver those who through fear of death were all their lifetime subject to bondage.

Do not fear death and do not be sin-conscious, Jesus is coming for those eagerly waiting on Jesus to return.

John 6:67-69 Then Jesus said to the Twelve, do you also wish to go away? Then Simon Peter answered Him, Lord, to whom shall we go? **You have *the* Words of eternal life. And we have believed and have known that You are the Christ (the Messiah), the Son of the living God.**

If you have received Jesus, it is an insult to say, "you are an old sinner saved by grace" and deny the Lord's sacrifice for all sin. **"You were an old sinner but now you are saved by Grace"**.

You are either a sinner or a Saint.
You cannot be both.
Or the Resurrection of Jesus was for naught.

The word "Saints" is <u>not</u> used in the New Testament <u>until the Resurrection of Jesus and then is used 60 times</u>. The change in wording is an important demarcation, Jesus either died for the entire universe of sin and broken covenants or we are still carrying our separation from GOD. You cannot be "an old sinner saved by grace". You are either a sinner or a Saint. If you are a Believer now, you WERE an old sinner but now you are a Saint saved by the grace of Jesus Christ.

The Grace of GOD is what you receive to change you from a sinner to a Saint. You cannot earn or deserve grace, it is a gift, or grace is not grace. And it is arrogance <u>to think that you have sins that the sacrifice of Jesus did not take care of at His death</u> and resurrection. Listen to the Apostle Paul speak to the calling of those who are part of the church.

1st Corinthians 1:2-3 To the church of God that is in Corinth, to those sanctified in Christ Jesus, <u>called "to be" saints</u> together with all those who in every place call upon the name of our Lord Jesus Christ, both their Lord and ours: Grace to you and peace from God, our Father, and the Lord Jesus Christ.

Called "to be" Saints gives Believers the power "to do" what Jesus has already "done". It is empowering to know that Jesus changed us from sinners to "Saints". We need to know "What Jesus Has done." to receive confidence in Jesus for the power "to do" acts of kindness, GOD has planned for Believers to do. Believers are sent into the world as Jesus was sent into the world to preach the Gospel, cast out devils, and heal the sick, you can't do those things if you are an "old sinner". Believers are "Saintified" or sanctified, think about the use of an extension cord that **when hooked up to Jesus**, delivers the power of the Lord to Believers to live the abundant life stopping the thief from stealing, killing, and destroying. *John 10:10*

John 14:12-14 "Truly, truly, I say to you, whoever believes in me <u>will also do the works that I do</u>; **and greater works than these will he do, because I am going to the Father**. Whatever you ask in my name, **this I will do**, that the Father may be glorified in the Son. If you ask me anything in my name, I will do it.

Ephesians 1:3-4 Blessed *be* the God and Father of our Lord Jesus Christ, **who has blessed (past tense) us <u>with all spiritual blessings</u> in heavenly** *places* **in Christ**: According as he hath chosen us in him before the foundation of the world, that we should be holy and without blame before him in love:

To further illustrate this analogy: Look at John 15:5 When you are the branch and you are hooked to Jesus, the vine, you can bear fruit, and nothing is impossible.

Conclusion to Section 3.

Galatians 1:3-5 Grace *be* to you and peace from God the Father, and *from* our Lord Jesus Christ, Who gave himself for our sins, **that he might deliver us from <u>this present evil world</u>**, according to the will of God and our Father: To whom *be* glory for ever and ever. Amen.

Chapter 9

GOD's word is
the Beginning of all life.

This chapter is filled with scripture revealing how GOD designed the world systems to operate with a foundation of love and how sin has perverted the good to look evil and evil to look good. <u>When anyone operates the Systems</u> **installed in the world by GOD** <u>the results are good</u> and when anyone perverts GOD's design and uses their own design, they reap a man-made result. GOD cares about people and only does good for people and wants His children to also love one another and do good to people.

The Bible is GOD's word and GOD's word is GOD. *<u>John 1:1-3</u>* GOD's word is Spiritual in nature and **when GOD's word is spoken,** it is good for controlling the Believers environment, both Spiritual and natural. GOD's word is not carnal or based on seeing, feeling, hearing, smelling, or tasting for its proof. **GOD's word is proven by what was created by GOD's word; the universe, the earth, the human body, and everything that has life was created and reproduces according to GOD's creative words.**

Evil is the only thing GOD did not make, evil was a product of rebellion against GOD **through choices of mankind's free-will,** first by Lucifer and secondly by Adam and Eve. Evil is man-made and demonic influenced. Its result is selfish in actions and ends in death.

Wisdom from Above
or influence from the enemy.

Scripture is the inspired word of GOD and GOD's word is good for <u>instruction, correction, rebuke,</u> or <u>teaching</u>. As you read the New Testament and especially the instructions <u>after the Resurrection of our Savior and the giving of "GOD, the Holy Spirit" to Believers,</u> GOD's word concentrates on <u>positive results for actions of good</u> and negative results for selfish acts. The motivation for all actions is: wise or foolish, good, or selfish, giving or hoarding, or divinely inspired or demonically influenced.

The scriptural instructions were written to Believers to point out right and wrong, truth and lies, selfish or giving, evil or good "choices". GOD's word will point out the proper path and what happens to you if you go down the right or the wrong path. If you choose a self-centered path the consequences **are not punishment from GOD** but are results from acting on a plan <u>not</u> blessed by GOD.

GOD said, "This day, I have set before you blessing and cursing, life, or death. **<u>Choose Life</u>**… Deuteronomy 30:19

Peace is the default atmosphere of the abundant life and <u>chaos, strife, and worry</u> are against everything GOD's word instructs. The Bible describes the engineering of life and its principles from gravity, love, lust, and more. Listen to the next scriptures that explain the principles in the Bible. These principles, when followed **will deliver the abundant life** or if **<u>not</u> followed** will rebuke or correct you through sorrow or consequences.

All scripture is from GOD and is GOD and is good for <u>teaching</u>, <u>correcting</u>, <u>training</u>, and <u>rebuke</u>. **GOD does not punish or tempt Believers**; His word is principled, blessed, and good. The non-blessed side of the GOD's <u>principles for living</u> **restrict the result to a man-made outcome or consequence**. Think about the GOD blessed side of the following series of scriptures and notice the consequences for actions, the scriptures warn against.

2nd Timothy 3:16-17 All Scripture is breathed out by God and profitable for <u>teaching</u>, for <u>reproof</u>, for <u>correction</u>, and for <u>training in righteousness</u>, **that the <u>man of God</u> may be complete, <u>equipped for every good work.</u>**

Next, receive your wisdom from above and live right, doing good, with humility. Notice the positivity of this principle.

James 3:13-18 Are there any among you who are really wise and understanding? <u>Then you should show your wisdom by living right</u>. You should **do what is good with humility.** <u>A wise person does not boast.</u>

<u>**Next**, consider others before yourself,</u> **<u>do not live in the grips of lust and chaos</u>**. Notice the prideful actions that do not carry the Lord's blessing.

If you are **selfish and have bitter jealousy in your hearts**, you have no reason to boast. Your boasting is a lie that hides the truth. That kind of "wisdom" <u>does not come from God</u>. That "wisdom" comes from the world. <u>It is not spiritual.</u> **It is from the devil.** <u>Where there is jealousy and selfishness, there will be confusion and every kind of evil. (Strife of all kinds)</u>

Next, wisdom is ready to do good for others and peace follows them. Another positive principle.

But <u>the wisdom that comes from God</u> **is like this**: First, it is <u>pure.</u> It is also <u>peaceful, gentle, and easy to please</u>. This wisdom is always ready <u>to help people who have trouble and to do good for others</u>. This wisdom is always fair and honest. **People who work for peace in a peaceful way get the blessings that come from right living**.

Next, the Peace of GOD <u>will keep your heart</u> when you think on these things.

Philippians 4:7-9 And <u>the peace of God</u> which passes all understanding shall keep your hearts and minds through Christ Jesus. Finally, my brothers, whatever things are <u>true</u>, whatever things *are* <u>honest</u>, whatever *things are* <u>right</u>, whatever *things are* <u>pure</u>, whatever *things are* <u>lovely</u>, whatever *things are* <u>of good report</u>; if *there is* <u>any virtue</u> and if *there is* <u>any praise</u>, **think on these things**. Do those things <u>which you have also learned and received and heard and **seen in me**</u>. And **<u>the God of peace shall be with you</u>**.

Next, for as a <u>man thinks</u>, **so is he**, and <u>out of his heart</u> his **mouth speaks**. This scripture reveals both good and evil and reveals that if you hear a person speaking evil out of his mouth <u>he has evil in his heart</u> and vice versus.

Luke 6:45 A **good man** out of the **good treasure of his heart** <u>brings forth the good</u>. And an **evil man** out of the **evil treasure** of his <u>heart brings forth the evil</u>. **For out of the abundance of the heart his mouth speaks.**

Next, receive your <u>desires from GOD, based on loving people,</u> and not the desires from the lusts of your body that <u>will keep you in chaos</u>. This next scripture lays out a list of the worst possible treasure of a heart for those **<u>not</u> being led** <u>by the Spirit of GOD</u>.

Galatians 5:18-25 But if you are led by the Spirit, <u>you are not under the law.</u>

Now the works of the flesh <u>are evident</u>: <u>sexual immorality, impurity, sensuality, idolatry, sorcery, enmity, strife, jealousy, fits of anger, rivalries, dissensions, divisions, envy, drunkenness, orgies, and things like these</u>. I warn you, as <u>I warned you before</u>, that **those who do such things <u>will not</u> inherit the kingdom of God.**

GOD has instructed before and now again <u>do not do these works of the flesh</u> but **seek to follow Jesus and love others as Jesus has loved us**.

Next, GOD's design of the world is powered by love, joy, peace, and more. This scripture reveals the actions that promote the "Abundant Life".

But the fruit of the Spirit <u>is love, joy, peace, patience, kindness, goodness, faithfulness, gentleness, self-control</u>; against such things there is no law. And those **who belong to Christ Jesus** <u>have crucified the flesh with its passions and desires</u>. If we live by the Spirit, let us also **keep in step with the Spirit**.

Next, corrupt talk is against the direction of the Holy Spirit and <u>does not edify</u>. This scripture shows both the positive side from GOD's designed systems and the systems of mankind <u>not blessed by GOD</u>.

Ephesians 4:29-30 **Let no corrupting** <u>talk come out of your mouths</u>, but **only such as is good for building up**, as fits the occasion, that it may **give grace to those who hear**<u>. And do not grieve the Holy Spirit of God, by whom you were sealed for the day of redemption.</u>

Next, actions based on **toxic emotions** are always against GOD's plan and kindness and love always please GOD.

Ephesians 4:31 Let all bitterness and wrath and anger and clamor and slander be put away from you, along with all malice. **Be kind to one another**, tenderhearted, forgiving one another, as God in Christ forgave you.

Next, do not allow your heart to become calloused and your mind alienated from GOD because at the end you will be separated from GOD.

Ephesians 4:17-22 Now this I say and testify in the Lord, that you must no longer walk as the (un-believers) Gentiles do, **in the futility of their minds**. They are darkened in their understanding, **alienated from the life of God** because of the ignorance that is in them, due to **their hardness of heart**. They have become callous and have given themselves up to sensuality, greedy to practice every kind of impurity.

Next, put off the old life and renew your mind and **put on Christ's Life**.

Ephesians 4:23-24 But that is not the way you learned Christ!—assuming that you have heard about him and were taught in him, **as the truth is in Jesus**, to put off your old self, which belongs to your former manner of life and **is corrupt through deceitful desires**, and to be renewed in the spirit of your minds, and **to put on the new self**, created after **the likeness of God** in true righteousness and holiness.

Next, give no opportunity to the Devil, be angry but do not sin. Again, this scripture has both the positive action when acting from GOD's word and the negative result for evil actions.

Ephesians 4:25-28 Therefore, having put away falsehood, let each one of you speak the truth with his neighbor, for we are members one of another (Believers are the Body and Bride of Christ). **Be angry and do not sin**; do not let the sun go down on your anger, and give no opportunity to the devil.

Let the thief no longer steal, but rather let him labor, doing honest work with his own hands, **so that he may have something to share with anyone in need.**

Next, this scripture is a revelation of what "GOD, the Holy Spirit" living inside Believers **can do and be**. Live life in the power of "GOD, the Holy Spirit" in your inner being **by faith in what Jesus has done. The Believer must act**, GOD will not act without the Believer, **because of mankind's free-will**.

Ephesians 3:14-21 For this reason I bow my knees before the Father, from whom every family in heaven and **on earth** is named, that according to the riches of his glory he may grant you to be **strengthened with power through his Spirit in your inner being,** so that Christ may dwell in your hearts through faith—that you, being rooted and grounded in love, may have strength to comprehend with all the saints what is the breadth and length and height and depth, and **to know the love of Christ** that surpasses knowledge, that you may be filled with all **the fullness of God**.

Next, now to "GOD, the Holy Spirit" (*inside Believers*), to Him be glory in the church **according to the power at work within Believers**.

Now to him who is able to do far more abundantly than all that we ask or think, **according to the power at work within us**, to him be glory in the church and in Christ Jesus throughout all generations, forever and ever. Amen.

Next, **guard what goes into your heart**, for what is in your heart will come out your mouth and can defile you.

Matthew 15:17-20 Do you **not see** that whatever goes into the mouth passes into the stomach and is expelled? But what comes out of the mouth **proceeds from the heart**, and **this defiles a person**. For out of the heart **come evil thoughts**, murder, adultery, sexual immorality, theft, false witness, slander. These are what defile a person. But to eat with unwashed hands does not defile anyone."

Section 2.

Now here are more examples of scripture concentrating on **Divine influence** or Demonic or self-centered influence.

Spiritual influence

James 3:13 Who is wise and understanding among you? By his good conduct let him show his works in the meekness of wisdom.

Demonic or self-centered influence

James 3:14 But if you have **bitter jealousy and selfish ambition** in your hearts, do not boast and be false to the truth.

James 3:15 **This is not the wisdom** that comes down from above, but is **earthly, unspiritual, demonic**.

Demonic or Self-centered influence

James 3:16 For where <u>jealousy and selfish ambition exist,</u> there will be disorder and **every vile practice. (Strife of every kind)**

Spiritual influence with motivation of love

James 3:17 But the wisdom <u>from above</u> is **first pure**, then **peaceable, gentle, open to reason, full of mercy and good fruits, impartial and sincere.**

James 3:18 And a <u>harvest of righteousness is sown in peace</u> by **those <u>who make peace.</u>**

<u>Demonic and self-centered thoughts and actions</u>

Galatians 5:19-21 **Now the works of the flesh <u>are evident</u>**: sexual Immorality, impurity, sensuality, idolatry, sorcery, enmity, strife, jealousy, fits of anger, rivalries, dissensions, divisions, envy, drunkenness, orgies, and things like these. **I warn you, as I warned you before, that those who do such things will not inherit the kingdom of God.**

Spiritual influence

Galatians 5:22-25 But **<u>the fruit of the Spirit</u> is love, joy, peace, faithfulness patience, kindness, goodness, faithfulness, gentleness, self-control</u>**; against such things there is no law. And those who belong to Christ Jesus have crucified the flesh with its passions and desires. **If we live by the Spirit, let us also keep in step with the Spirit.**

Did you see the instructions for good and the warnings of living against the instructions from GOD's word. **GOD's word will wash you clean and show you the light of life**. Following Jesus will lead you <u>away from chaos and **into peace**</u>, <u>out of darkness and **into light**</u>.

When you find your-self in chaos and troubled, **<u>STOP</u>** and realize you are in the wrong place and leave that place in your mind and capture your thoughts and replace those thoughts with a promise from "GOD, the Holy Spirit" and <u>GOD's word will lead you into peace</u> and away from chaos.

<u>**Section 3.**</u> Putting GOD's word to work in our lives will power confidence in Christ living in Believers.

** When you're not hearing GOD,
Go to the word, it is GOD. **

What does a Believer do when <u>they **do not know** that they are hearing from GOD</u> for a plan for the day or for a special moment. Answer, there is a "general" word from GOD for all our lives, "Love GOD, and love your neighbors, family, and co-workers more than you love yourself" and <u>let the peace of GOD rule in your heart</u> as you choose the kindness you distribute in your day and the witness of your love of GOD for Mankind.

If you concentrate on making everyone's task easier and day better with words of encouragement or acts of kindness, you are on the right track. Ask GOD constantly and expect "GOD, the Holy Spirit" to tell you about the spiritual and physical needs of your family, acquaintances, and people in your day that you can help with a word or a deed.

When you understand GOD's grace, is the answer to human weakness, Believers can react to an obstacle to fulfilling GOD's plan for their day with GOD's sufficiency in a time of need. Peace is your first objective. Do not lose sight of the warning to **not** be double minded, be sure you are "One with GOD".

If a Believer is in a national calamity and the need is desperate to hear from GOD, the principle is the same because **GOD does not change,** and His word does not change. **Your only hope** is to change how you are looking at the calamity. GOD is available.

In the New Covenant, James 4:6-8 But he gives more grace. Wherefore he says, **God resists the proud**, but gives grace to the humble. **Submit yourselves therefore to God.** Resist the devil, and he will flee from you. **Draw near to God**, and he will draw near to you. Cleanse *your* hands, you sinners; and purify *your* hearts, *you* double minded.

Remember, it is the Believer's faith in GOD's faith that will power Believers to accomplish GOD's plan. Believers must believe GOD, believe His word, and know His love for the Saints and the **un**believers.

Grace for daily living can't be earned or deserved but it must be found (seek and you will find). Think about this, Jesus faced what seemed an insurmountable task in GOD's plan to reconcile mankind (death on a cross) and Jesus asked Father GOD if there was another way, other than His death and separation from GOD but the answer to His prayer (3 times in Matthew's record) **the answer** was GOD's grace would be sufficient. (Hebrews 2:7-10)

Hebrews 2:7-10 You made him for a little while lower than the angels; you have crowned him with glory and honor, putting everything in subjection under his feet." Now in putting everything in subjection to him, he left nothing outside his control. At present, we do not yet see everything in subjection to him. But we see him who for a little while was made lower than the angels, namely <u>Jesus, crowned with glory and honor because of the suffering of death</u>, so that **by <u>the grace of God he might taste death for everyone.</u>** <u>For it was fitting that he,</u> **<u>for whom and by whom all things exist</u>**<u>, in bringing many sons to glory, should make the founder of their salvation</u> **<u>perfect through suffering</u>**.

There are times when you're offering of kindness to "the hateful" will require the Grace of God to stomach their response to your attempt to minister kindness or witness. Do not take offense at the "hateful reaction"; you are being led by GOD, "Praise GOD" and go forth to the next opportunity; you have planted a seed and now it is up to GOD to have someone else to water.

Example, if you felt led to give a dollar to a beggar at a corner, and the man looked at your gift and at you and with disdain said, "what do you expect me to buy with this?" you might be caught off guard, and feel bad for a moment about your gift, before realizing that you did what you were led to do, so <u>shake off his response</u> and go on to find another act of kindness. Father GOD is pleased with you hearing and acting on the word from "GOD, the Holy Spirit". Your attempt at kindness is a seed planted. **Alert**, God will not put every beggar on your heart for you to minister, but **when God moves you**, minister with a word, or gift as an act for GOD.

Note about **un**believers. Hearing the word of GOD wakes up in <u>un</u>believers <u>the faith to want a relationship with GOD</u>. GOD gave every man "the measure of faith" **to know GOD**. It is one of mankind's faculties like sight, hearing, touch, taste, smell, and <u>faith to know GOD</u>.

As Believers, we must be likeminded with "the mind of Christ" in our Spirit and act on "the faith" Believers have in <u>the faith of Jesus Christ</u> and Father GOD. Believers know Jesus with His faith completed all the works of GOD restoring GOD's plan and benefits for your life.

Many Believers do not believe they have faith to do any mighty works and <u>that is right</u>, **without Christ, or the "mind of Christ" united with our mind**, <u>we can do nothing</u> in the Spiritual realm to change the physical realm. **"But GOD"**, is with us, inside us, and will never leave us and **Believers are mighty through GOD**.

<u>Listen to these scriptures and **power up**</u>.

Mark 16:15-18 And he said to them, "Go into all the world and proclaim the gospel to the whole creation. Whoever believes and is baptized will be saved, but whoever does not believe will be condemned. **And these signs will accompany those who believe: in my name** they will **<u>cast out demons</u>**; they will **<u>speak in new tongues</u>**; they will pick up serpents with their hands; and if they drink any deadly poison, **it will not hurt them**; <u>**they will lay their hands on the sick, and they will recover**</u>."

1ˢᵗ Corinthians 6:17 <u>But he who is joined to the Lord</u> becomes <u>one spirit with him.</u>

Galatians 5:22-25 But <u>the fruit of the Spirit</u> is: love, joy, peace, long-suffering, kindness, goodness, faith, meekness, self-control; against such things there is no law. But those belonging to Christ <u>have crucified the flesh with *its* passions and lusts. If we live in *the* Spirit, let us also walk in *the* Spirit.</u>

1ˢᵗ Corinthians 13:10-13 Charity has patience, <u>is</u> kind; charity is not envious, is not vain, is not puffed up; does not behave indecently, does not seek her own, <u>is not easily provoked,</u> **thinks no evil**.

Charity does not rejoice in unrighteousness, <u>but rejoices in the truth</u>, quietly covers all things, believes all things, hopes all things, endures all things.

<u>These verses confirm the Lord's new Commandment, Love others as I have loved you with actions proving your commitment to love.</u>

"GOD, the Holy Spirit" is inside Believers, It is arrogance to know this and <u>not</u> speak to GOD, daily.

Believers do not always ask, seek, and knock at the door of "GOD, the Holy Spirit' to plan their day, <u>but they should</u>. A Believer <u>has a perfect Spirit</u> **created in the exact image of GOD**, in a body programmed with selfish habits. The Believer's mind must be renewed by the washing of the word of GOD and for the best results submit to leadership from "GOD, the Holy Spirit".

"GOD, the Holy Spirit" may not always give you a specific plan for your day but taking time to ask the Holy Spirit if there is a specific plan will confirm your direction to a General word or the Specific word for a moment in time.

<u>Leave the slavery of the past to go with the freedom of the future with GOD</u>. Listen to the Apostle Paul describe this phenomenon.

Romans 6:4-6 Therefore we are buried with him by baptism into death: that **like as Christ was raised up from the dead**

by the glory of the Father, even so we also should walk in newness of life. For if we have been **planted together** in the likeness of his death, we shall be also *in the likeness* of *his* resurrection: Knowing this, that our old man is crucified with *him,* that the (our) body of sin might be destroyed, that henceforth we should not serve sin.(old programming)

Romans 6:7 For he, **who died** has been justified from sin. But if we died with Christ, **we believe that we** shall also live with Him, knowing that when Christ was raised from *the* dead, He dies no more; **death no longer has dominion over Him**. (Nor over Believers)

The freedom of intimately knowing Jesus Christ and to live in the peace and love of Christ is the Believers eternal destiny on earth. You must know that your old habits are **not** in your best interests and allowing Christ to live in you, in every thought and action will deliver better results.

Get rid of your stinking thinking. Your "sinful nature" is gone and buried when you are Born-again, but your mental programming is still selfish, and full of bad habits. The Believer must renew your programming to the freedom of being a child of GOD. Believers must put on "the new man" and put off "the old man's" propensity to sin. "The old man" is selfish and loves himself. **"The New Man" loves GOD and others more significantly than himself.**

Romans 6:1-2 Are we to continue in sin that grace may abound? **By no means! (GOD forbid),** How can we who died to sin (the sin nature) still live in it (after receiving the "Nature of GOD"?)

Listen to the Apostle Paul tell us more about putting on our new self and keeping our minds focused on operating our lives with the "Fruit of the Spirit" and not the works of the flesh.

Put On your New Self

Colossians 3:1-17 If then you have been raised with Christ, seek the things that are above, where Christ is, seated at the right hand of God. **Set your minds** on things that are above, **not** on things that are on earth. For you have died, and your life is hidden with Christ in God. When Christ, **who is your life**, appears then you also will appear with him in glory. (Not a place but "Doxa" a physical appearance.)

Put to death therefore **what is earthly in you**: sexual immorality, impurity, passion, evil desire, and covetousness, which is idolatry. Because of these the wrath of God is coming. In these you too once walked when you were living in them. But now you must put them all away: anger, wrath, malice, slander, and obscene talk from your mouth. Do not lie to one another, seeing that you have put off the old self with its practices and **have put on the new self, which is being renewed in knowledge after the image of its creator**.

Notice. It is the renewing of your mind to the knowledge of GOD and of your new relationship with "GOD, the Holy Spirit" that powers your new life, Christ living in you. And the Apostle Paul continues with GOD's destiny for Believers **loving others more than you love yourself** without judgement of age, color, gender, denomination, or political party.

Here there is not Greek nor Jew, circumcised or uncircumcised, barbarian, Scythian, slave, or free; but Christ is all, and in all. **Put on then, as God's chosen ones, holy and beloved, compassionate hearts, kindness, humility, meekness, and**

patience, bearing with one another and, if one has a complaint against another, forgiving each other; as the Lord has forgiven you, so you also must forgive. And above all these put-on love, which binds everything together in perfect harmony. And let the peace of Christ rule in your hearts, to which indeed you were called in one body. And be thankful. *Colossians 3:1-15*

Note, for those who do not hear from GOD verbally or in your mind, you can hear from GOD through making decisions based on the peace in your heart that you experience as you choose your options. **If you have the peace of GOD in your heart move with the choice of action that brings peace**. Also, if the motivation of your actions and the purpose of your heart is to do everything all in the "Name of Jesus" you will not be far off base.

Let the word of Christ dwell in you richly, teaching and admonishing one another in all wisdom, singing psalms and hymns and spiritual songs, with thankfulness in your hearts to God. And whatever you do, in word or deed, **do everything in the name of the Lord Jesus**, giving thanks to God the Father through him.

Colossians 3:14-15 And above all these things *put on* **love**, which is *the* bond of perfectness. And let the peace of God rule in your hearts, to which you also are called in one body, and be thankful.

Studying the word of GOD will give you a picture of what happens when you follow GOD's word and what happens when you follow another path **not** blessed with GOD's word. Choose life through GOD's word, His life, and His Spirit.